Florence Marryat

A broken Blossom

Vol. II

Florence Marryat

A broken Blossom
Vol. II

ISBN/EAN: 9783337052089

Printed in Europe, USA, Canada, Australia, Japan

Cover: Foto ©ninafisch / pixelio.de

More available books at **www.hansebooks.com**

A BROKEN BLOSSOM.

A Novel.

BY

FLORENCE MARRYAT,

AUTHOR OF "LOVE'S CONFLICT," ETC., ETC., ETC.

IN THREE VOLUMES.
VOL. II.

London:
SAMUEL TINSLEY & CO.,
10, SOUTHAMPTON STREET, STRAND.
1879.

[*All Rights Reserved.*]

CONTENTS OF VOL. II.

CHAPTER	PAGE
I. THE VENETIAN GLASS	1
II. ARTHUR THRALE	36
III. THE SECRET	64
IV. THE DENOUEMENT	89
V. CURED	116
VI. TWO SERPENTS	136
VII. ALL FOR TESSIE	162
VIII. A REVELATION	194
IX. CHARLIE	223

A BROKEN BLOSSOM.

CHAPTER I.

THE VENETIAN GLASS.

THE *goûter* was laid in a long narrow room, which evidently had once been a banqueting hall. Remnants of exquisitely stained glass still ornamented its windows, although the ravages made in them by time had been replaced by ordinary white panes. Tall, straight-backed chairs, carved in black oak, and furnished with green cushions, the embossed velvet covering of which was both faded and rent, stood at the table for our accommodation, whilst from the panelling of the walls looked down upon us an almost obliterated collection of the Baron's ancestors.

Although the summer sun was shining through the windows, casting rainbow lights of ruby and violet and amber over the damask tablecloth, and the roses and clematis were hanging in clusters about the casement, there was a weird unearthly feeling about this chamber that made me shudder.

An artist would have fallen into raptures over the old oaken floors and wainscoting; the leash of wolfhounds that lay stretched out blinking in the sunshine, and watching their master's eye as for a revelation; the fragments of stained glass; the blackened ancestors. But to me, the aspect of the whole place spelt *Ruin*, and I feared lest our host should read my feelings in my face.

That did not, however, seem likely. There

he sat at the head of the table, dispensing his simple hospitality as though he had been entertaining crowned heads at a royal banquet. He made no apology for the repast he offered us. It was the best he had to give, and he credited us with too much good taste to wish it better. When he pledged us in the *vin ordinaire* of the country, poured into the most delicate of Venetian wineglasses, the slender stems of which were encircled by a tiny twist of blue and their bowls dotted with specks of gold, he might have been a prince drinking to his courtiers in a vintage of fabulous value. Those glasses alone were a marvel in themselves, and, mere fragmentary remains as they were of a past glory, told tales of what that glory must have been.

I thought, as I balanced mine between my finger and thumb, what an exquisite specimen of workmanship it was, and how I should like to possess it and keep it in my bedroom for my own delectation, to place the first violets of spring in, or the first lilies of summer. It looked so much too fragile and precious to be handled for ordinary purposes.

I was thinking thus, when some one spoke to me—the Baron himself, perhaps—and I was startled into letting the wineglass slip from my hand. It struck the table and was shivered into a thousand fragments. I blushed to scarlet. Had the accident happened in the house of an ordinary host, I should have thought little of it, but to Monsieur le Baron, who was so poor! I tried to stammer out an apology, but the words failed on my lips. Mr. Lovett saw my embarrassment, and laughed heartily at it. I had already commenced to find out that his notions were beyond his means, and that he did not sympathise very strongly with any ideas of economy or restriction.

Tessie and Ange looked as concerned as I did. The Baron alone continued the conversation as if nothing had occurred. But I could not allow the matter to rest there.

'Monsieur!' I said, 'I am so *very* sorry. I was only just thinking how beautiful this little glass was, and how much too delicate to hold anything except spring flowers.'

'Then I am sorry also, mademoiselle! But was that the only one of the pattern you admire? Cannot we find another that will do as well to hold your blossoms?'

I remonstrated with this proposal, although he made Denise bring the remainder of her stock of glasses and spread them out upon the table before us. There they sparkled in their prismatic hues of blue and red and gold, and their elegant fragile shapes and twisted stems. But I refused to do more than look at them. I was too clumsy, I averred, to be the possessor of such delicate things. One such injury to art, as I had done that day, was enough for me!

The Baron did not press the point, but, as we had finished luncheon, he unleashed his hounds, and, calling them to follow us, led the way into the tangled wilderness he called his garden. As we passed the stables and coachhouse, I perceived that they were shut up and empty. Their owner had not even the means sufficient to keep a riding-horse for himself. As I glanced at his noble bearing and pictured the luxury in which he had probably been reared, I did feel intense pity for his lonely and impoverished condition.

'We must not forget the object for which you honoured the château with a visit,' he said as we traversed the grounds, which were of some extent, 'which was to ascertain if any life remains in the poor old organ; but I must show you my pet first.'

He pushed aside the trailing branches of the bushes as he spoke, and led the way up to a large cave, or den, surrounded by a palisade of stout wood. Inside it, running restlessly up and down, was a splendid wolf of the Piron breed. We girls rather shrunk back as we came in sight of the animal.

'You need not be in the slightest degree alarmed, mesdemoiselles,' said our host; 'for the palings are very strong, and "L'Empereur" is wonderfully tame!' And, in proof of his assertion, the Baron walked up to the palisades and stroked the wolf's head. '*Eh bien, mon ami!*' he exclaimed, 'are you glad to see me again? It is some time since I have paid you a visit, *mon pauvre Empereur.*'

'Monsieur, where did you get him?' asked Ange.

'I shot his mother in the forest, Mademoiselle Ange, two years ago. Empereur was then a little cub, of perhaps a month or six weeks old. He was easily caught, and I brought him home and kept him in the château, until he took to biting the heels of Denise rather too vigorously as she went about her work, and I was compelled to have this apartment erected for him out of doors.'

'He is a strange pet to keep,' I observed.

'So several people have told me; but Empereur and I have sympathies in common. His estates, like mine, have been confiscated; for, since St. Pucelle has been a town, the wolves have been driven farther and farther back into the interior of the forest of Piron. Then he is solitary, and so am I; and his misfortunes make him savage, as mine have done to me; and we thirst in common, I think, for the blood of our enemies, and choose the night-time to moan over our wrongs. Is it not so, Empereur?' concluded the Baron, with a forced laugh, as he thrust his hand again between the open palings, and rubbed the head of his favourite.

'And a wolf is your family crest, is it not, monsieur?' I said, with a view to cover the Baron's last remark, which had made us all feel rather uncomfortable.

'True, mademoiselle. It was granted to be borne by my ancestor, Godefroi de Nesselrode, and his descendants, by one of the first Ducs de Nemours. The Duc and De Nesselrode were riding, unattended and unarmed, when an assassin made an attempt upon the life of the former. His first shot, however, failed; and, before he had time to fire a second time, my ancestor had leapt from his horse and flown at his throat, never leaving hold until he had strangled him where he lay. As a wolf will invariably fly at the throat of a man, if it is possible to do so, his princely master, the Duc de Nemours, was pleased to command that that animal should be carried as a crest upon the helmets of the De Nesselrodes from that time forward.'

'It was a very brave thing for your ancestor to do,' said Tessie.

'He could hardly have done anything else,' replied the Baron, quietly. 'But would it be agreeable to you now, mesdemoiselles, to try the organ we have spoken of?'

'Yes, yes; let us return to the house,' interposed Mr. Lovett. 'It is too hot to stand about, so early in the afternoon.'

The fact is, the old gentleman had made an excellent luncheon, and began to miss the nap which he invariably took at that hour of the day. So, his will being law to all of us, we retraced our footsteps to the château, and were introduced to what had originally been its private chapel. But what a desecration appeared to have taken place there!

The altar was disrobed and bare, and what

ornaments it had possessed had vanished. Over it hung a crucifix, covered with a layer of dust an inch in thickness. On one side was erected a little altar to the Virgin. Her statue still rested there, on a cloth of what had been white silk, now brown with dirt and age, with the yellow lace hanging from it in tattered fragments. A dusty wreath of artificial flowers stood before it, and a little lamp which still held the rancid remains of oil. A row of oak benches was on either side the altar; but, beyond what I have mentioned, and a few votive offerings of little value which hung against the wall, all traces of this place having been one of prayer had disappeared. As we entered it, Ange gave vent to an exclamation of dismay.

'Oh, monsieur! why do you not have this chapel properly cleaned, and kept in order——?' But there the child stopped, remembering his poverty.

'To what intent, mademoiselle?' he asked her.

'Oh, because—because—it *has* been so beautiful!' she replied. 'Papa, what would we not give to have this chapel carried down into St. Pucelle, and to use it for our services, instead of the schoolroom? Does it not seem ten thousand pities that it should be wasted like this?'

Mr. Lovett had already ensconced himself on the corner of one of the benches, and put two cushions at his back, preparatory to passing into the land of dreams.

'A great pity, my little maid,' he answered, sleepily. 'But I am not sure how De Nesselrode would approve of your carrying it off, nevertheless.' And then he gave two huge yawns, and closed his eyes.

'It will all be restored some day,' I said cheerily, 'and made more beautiful, perhaps, than it was before.'

'Do you think so, mademoiselle?' inquired the Baron of me.

'I hope so, monsieur. And what a fine organ! If its tone is only as good as its appearance, we shall have a treat.'

'It has not been touched for years,' he said, as he opened it, 'until I told Denise to dust it for you this morning.'

Tessie seated herself at the instrument, and commenced to play some passages from the 'Stabat Mater,' whilst I worked the bellows for her. The organ had been left to the tender mercies of so many winters, that its tone left a good deal to be desired. Still, it was a very fine instrument, and only required a few fires and regular practice to bring it once more into working order. I was wondering to myself what this visit would lead to, and if Tessie would receive an invitation to come up to the château and play the organ, until she had played herself into the owner's heart, when I found that the owner had crept round to the back of the instrument, and was standing beside the bellows and myself.

Ange was busily engaged setting the Virgin's altar in order, and dusting the ornaments with her pocket-handkerchief; Mr. Lovett was slumbering blissfully on the oaken seat, and the notes of the 'Mater Dolorosa' were still pealing out from under Tessie's skilful fingers.

As far as what we said or did was concerned, the Baron de Nesselrode and I might have been quite alone, and now was the opportunity, I thought, to put in a word for the future of my sweet Tessie and the man who stood beside me.

But it was he who commenced the conversation.

'Mademoiselle, why do you think that this ruined chapel will some day be restored?'

'Because I believe that when you *can* do it, you *will.*'

'But will that opportunity ever arise?'

'That I cannot say, Monsieur; neither have I the right to inquire. Only—I have been told——'

'*What?*'

'That you will not always be as you are now.'

I said the words timidly, but directly they had left my lips they sounded terribly bold, and I coloured under the conviction that they were so.

'Forgive me, monsieur,' I added; 'I should not have said that. I feel I have entrenched on your private affairs.'

'There is nothing to forgive, mademoiselle. I have ruined myself. The story is patent to all. It is also true that by a long course of privation I may regain my former position. But it is not at all likely.'

'Why not?'

In my interest and surprise I overlooked the fact that this question was entrenching still more upon his private affairs than the former remark had been.

'Because I think I shall return to Paris. I am sick and tired of the life I lead here, and am ready to sacrifice my future itself in order to break through the chains that keep me a prisoner in St. Pucelle.'

'Oh no! monsieur, you must be patient! You must not do that!'

What made me speak to this stranger in so unaccountable a manner?

Some sudden thought of Tessie, and that she would be left to pine in solitude in St. Pucelle, whilst the Baron was recklessly throwing away his last chances of respectability and honour in Paris, had put them into my mind and made me forget myself. I expected that my companion would be offended at my audacity, but he did not even look surprised.

'Why should I not do so?' he answered quietly; 'I live only for myself. No one cares what becomes of my future! It is mine to do as I will with; and this life is too intolerable to be endured for one's self alone.'

'You may not always be alone,' I said, thinking of the fair-haired woman divided from us only by the organ.

The Baron laughed incredulously.

'This is a pretty château, is it not, to bring a young lady home to, mademoiselle, and ask her to live upon roses? They smell sweet enough as they adorn your bosom, but you would not find them very satisfying as your daily food.'

At that I laughed also.

'No, indeed! Still, monsieur——'

'I wait the commands of mademoiselle——'

'Even if no one cares what becomes of your future, you have the honour and glory of the past in your keeping.'

He made no answer to this remark, and when I ventured to look up in his face I saw that he was biting his lips.

Whether he would have replied to me I know not, but at that moment the notes of the organ ceased, the bellows gave a great squeak, and Ange came laughing to ask us if she had not already made a great improvement in the appearance of the chapel.

'If Monsieur le Baron will only let me repair the altar-cloth and clean the ornaments it will make the whole place look different. And the organ sounds lovely, Tessie! I wish you could have heard it yourself from a little distance. Has it not been a pleasure to you to touch an organ again? You have never had an opportunity of playing on one since we were last in Brussels.'

'Yes, I have enjoyed it greatly,' replied Tessie. 'The notes are a little stiff from damp and disuse, and I do not think you worked the bellows very regularly, Hilda; but otherwise we have nothing like this in St. Pucelle. I only wish I could carry it away in my pocket.'

'If it is really a pleasure to you to use the instrument, mademoiselle, I trust you will regard it as your own,' said the Baron, 'and play on it as often as may be convenient to yourself. The key of the chapel is always left in the hands of Denise, and I will give her orders to see that it is kept in a fit state for your accommodation.'

'Oh, that will be delightful!' cried Ange, who was much more enthusiastically disposed than her sister; 'and I may have charge of the rest of it, may I not, monsieur—and keep the altar dressed with flowers, as I do for papa on Sundays?'

'Anything that Mademoiselle Ange chooses to do, she will find me grateful for,' replied the Baron. 'And Mademoiselle Marsh, too, I hope this is not the last time she will honour the château with her presence.'

'Oh! I will come when Tessie does,' I answered, laughing, 'to blow the bellows, though I have not incurred much gratitude for the exertions I have undergone on her behalf to-day.'

'Mademoiselle Lovett says nothing herself,' remarked De Nesselrode.

'Because it depends so entirely upon papa,' replied Tessie, blushing; 'and he has so many engagements in the parish and otherwise, that I do not know when he may be able to bring us up to the château again.'

And then we all remembered the difficulties that lay in the way of three young, unmarried ladies making any practical use of an organ that stood in the residence of an unprotected bachelor.

'Papa *must* bring us up; we will *make* him!' exclaimed Ange, as she unceremoniously squatted upon her sleeping father's knee and kissed him back to consciousness. 'Papa! wake up! You've been asleep a great deal too long—and tell us how soon you will bring us to the château again to play upon this lovely organ.'

'Eh! eh! what?' said Mr. Lovett, as he started up and realised where he was. 'Why, you little puss! you are enough to frighten a man into a fit. What is it you want? Is it time to go home?'

'Pretty nearly, papa, and quite time for you to wake up and make yourself agreeable. Monsieur le Baron says we may practise on his organ every day; but you will have to bring us to the château. Will you come to-morrow again?'

'No, no, no! How can I come to-morrow? It is Saturday, and I shall have my sermon to think over and prepare, and a dozen other things to do,' replied Mr. Lovett, taking the girl's words seriously. 'Besides, it is such a hill to climb! My breath is too short to accomplish it often. If you want to run about the château as if it belonged to you, you must get some old woman to chaperon you—Mrs. Carolus, for instance, or Mrs. Petherton.'

'Or Miss Markham. I'm sure she is old enough,' interposed Ange, with a most unusual degree of acrimony for her.

'Miss Markham is an unmarried lady, my dear: she would be of no more use in satisfying the exigencies of etiquette than yourself. However, we will talk over this scheme later, for it is really time that we were moving homewards now. Baron, we have to thank you for your excellent hospitality, and to hope you will soon give us the opportunity to return it. I shall see you this evening, perhaps, if you have nothing better to do.'

'Without fail, monsieur,' replied the Baron, warmly; and then, when we girls had reassumed our walking attire, he accompanied us to the entrance of the château, and bid us farewell, with numerous entreaties that we would not allow many days to elapse before we came back to play upon the old organ again.

As we walked home together, Mr. Lovett informed us that the Baron de Nesselrode reminded him powerfully of the great friend and patron of his earlier days—the noble poet, of whom, *par excellence*, England has reason to be proud, Lord Amor.

'Amor was the most misunderstood and misjudged of all God's creatures,' he said warmly. 'He was afflicted with so mighty a genius and so keen a sensitiveness, that his mind could scarcely be said to be in a normal condition; and added to that, he possessed a temperament which left him open to every sort of temptation. I perceive much of his character reproduced in Armand de Nesselrode. Without possessing Amor's genius, which does not appear once in a century, he has yet a very poetical and imaginative brain, which in his enforced solitude is likely to produce a morbid condition of thought. We must induce him to mix amongst us as much as possible.'

'It is a pity he has not more love for reading, or else more companions of his own age,' I observed. 'Utter idleness is certain to make a man fall back upon vice for amusement.'

My trustee glanced at me keenly. Did he imagine I could possibly know more of the Baron's habits than he did?

'There is not much opportunity for the

practice of vice in St. Pucelle, my dear,' he observed.

'Is there not, sir? Then St. Pucelle must be a very uncommon sort of place. But, if all one hears is true, the Baron's great failing has been the love of gambling: and that form of vice is feasible wherever a pack of cards is to be procured.'

I fancied I had made Mr. Lovett quite angry by my insinuation against his friend.

'That is a hard judgment, my dear Hilda —harder than I like to hear proceed from the mouth of so young a woman. You must not think because poor De Nesselrode may occasionally while away the weary hours of his exile by a game of cards, that he has therefore necessarily not abandoned the fatal habit of gambling. There is no harm in a game of cards. I sometimes indulge in one myself; and I should be glad to hear you speak a little more charitably of your neighbours, my dear Hilda.' You are too young to be suspicious. Whatever our friends' faults may be, let us remember our own, and preserve a generous silence.'

I felt very small under this clerical rebuke, particularly as the girls were regarding their father as if he were a Solomon called to judgment, and proportionately disposed to censure my boldness.

'I did not intend to be uncharitable,' I answered humbly; 'and perhaps my experience of life has made me suspicious. But, at all events, I may say that I think it would be safer, under the circumstances, for the Baron to abandon cards altogether, even as a game.'

'He is the best judge of his own affairs,' replied Mr. Lovett, curtly; and then we started a pleasanter topic, and dropped the one in hand.

At the usual hour in the evening, Armand

de Nesselrode came. We heard his voice in the *salle*, although we did not see him, as the girls said it was their father's particular desire that he should not be disturbed after we had risen from the dinner-table, and left him to the enjoyment of his wine and cigar and the conversation of any friend who might look in upon him. But on this evening I felt particularly curious to learn what was going on in the *salle*. I could distinguish the gentlemen's voices as they laughed and talked with one another; but I wanted to see what they were about. The new-born interest I had conceived in the Baron's future prospects had much to do with my curiosity; because I thought, until I had some proof that he still practised it, I should never have the audacity to speak to him openly about giving up the amusement that had been his ruin.

So by-and-by I yawned, and rising, told Tessie and Ange that the day's expedition had tired me, and I should go to bed; at which announcement they laughed, and called me lazy, but raised no objection to the plan; and I reached my chamber, without either having offered to accompany me.

Madame Marmoret called after me, in her coarse voice, to know if I intended coming down again that evening; but I would not answer her. Madame and I were foes, although there had never been an open rupture between us. I disliked her insolence and familiarity too much to be civil to her; and she hated me because I took no notice of her rudeness.

It was ten o'clock as I entered my bed-room. The dear old carriage-clock was ticking away upon the mantelpiece to tell me so. I wrapped myself in a dark waterproof cloak, and throwing the hood over my head, passed through the French windows at the end of the corridor that led out into the garden, from which a door in the wall opened upon the road.

For a few moments I lingered at the flowerbeds, picking a blossom here and there, for fear the girls might follow me, and suspect the motive of my absence ; but no one came. So, plucking up my courage, I gently opened the garden-door, and crept noiselessly up the wooden steps that led to the *salle*. One window, half hidden by clustering tendrils of vine, abutted on the platform at the head of the steps, and through it the whole of the *salle* was visible.

It was as I had thought and feared. Mr. Lovett and the Baron were seated opposite to each other, with the green-shaded lamp between them, and their hands full of cards. The table was strewn with counters of various colours, and two or three little piles of money stood at my trustee's elbow. Even as I stood and gazed at them, afraid to breathe lest my presence should be discovered, I saw the Baron lose again, and add another coin to the heap on the other side the table, at which Mr. Lovett laughed, and exclaimed :

'*A la bonne fortune, mon cher.* Try again! It only requires perseverance to turn the shadiest luck.'

As I crept back to my bedchamber and prepared myself for rest, I felt very sick and miserable. I knew the world was full of wickedness and sorrow, but I never seemed so fully to have realised it as I did that night ; and I wished—oh, so truly!—that I were safe with *her* wherever she might be, and had finished the bitter task of learning the lesson of life. If I missed her at one time more than another, it was at such moments as these, when I felt confused and stupefied under the shock of discovering more sin and misery in the world than I had thought it capable of containing, and had no bosom to fly to for comfort and reassurance.

I hoped that neither Tessie nor Ange would ask to see me again that evening. I wanted to go to bed, and lose in sleep, if possible, the uncomfortable feelings that had taken possession of me. After which, I was not over-pleased, as may be supposed, to hear Madame Marmoret's voice demanding admittance at my door.

'You cannot come in, Madame, indeed! It is impossible! I am just about to step into my bed.'

'*Eh bien!* It is no concern of mine. Step into your bed, if it pleases you to do so. But I wish I had not taken the trouble to follow you upstairs, which I should not have done, except for the entreaties of Monsieur le Baron. In my day, a young woman was pleased to be taken notice of, especially if she did not deserve it; but 'tis all the same to me. I will go downstairs again, and tell Monsieur le Baron that you refuse me the entrance to your chamber.'

'Monsieur le Baron!' I repeated in surprise. 'What on earth has he to do with your being here?'

'Ah, I thought I would arouse your curiosity! We may be extremely modest and reserved, and not have a civil word to throw at our inferiors; but the name of a Baron is at all times better than that of a commoner, and likely to command more attention—is it not so?'

'Madame Marmoret, if you have a message of any importance for me, please to deliver it at once, and let me go to rest.'

'It is no message, then, but a packet, which I have been charged to deliver into your hands; and if you will not take it, I will just lay it in your doorway, and the first foot that comes past may smash it to pieces!'

Aggravated at the woman's impertinence, and curious to learn what a packet from the Baron could possibly contain for me, I opened the door, and received a small parcel carefully enveloped with paper.

'Is there no message to be taken back again?' demanded Madame Marmoret, grinning like a wicked old witch at me.

'None. I have no idea what the packet can hold.'

'Ah, you wish me to believe that, mademoiselle, of course! and when I was paid to deliver it, too! Well, I've done my duty, and you can do yours.'

And, with these words and a harsh laugh, Madame took her way downstairs again.

I carried the parcel eagerly to the light, and took off its manifold wrappings, when it disclosed an exquisitely-moulded Venetian vase of the most costly workmanship, and far superior to anything which we had seen at the Château des Roses that day. At first I could not believe that it was intended for me instead of Tessie; but a little card that fell out of the bowl reassured me. On it, beneath the printed words, 'Armand de Nesselrode,' was written, '*Pour les fleurs de Mademoiselle Hilda.*'

I felt very much pleased. As an acquisition alone, the Venetian vase would have delighted me; because I possessed a cultivated taste, and took keen interest in all specimens of art, ancient and modern.

It would stand on my mantelshelf, and be 'a joy for ever,' with its fragile loveliness and perfect grace of form.

But far above the value of his little gift, I hailed the evident goodwill of the giver. He had not taken my frank remarks in bad part. My vase was a proof that he was not offended with me. What opportunities, then, might I not hope to gain in the future, to warn him from pursuing the path which my own eyes had told me he still trod!

Before Madame had delivered my parcel, I was afraid lest the illegal means by which I had gained my knowledge might for ever prevent my making use of it. Now I felt no fear about it.

The Baron de Nesselrode had paved the way for me. He could not complain if I took advantage of his kindness to return it. He had given me a present, and he should receive one in return. If ever I were on the brink of offending him by my good advice, I would plead my little vase as an excuse for trying to return the kindness he had shown me in the only coin I possessed.

CHAPTER II.

ARTHUR THRALE.

THE sun was streaming down the narrow rocky street of St. Pucelle, in one long, unbroken line of light. I could hear the shrill voice of Madame Marmoret screaming to frighten away the pigeons, as they alighted on the line she had erected in the courtyard to hang her spotless caps and aprons on; and Tessie disturbed me in the midst of writing a long letter home—somehow, I found it difficult to get out of the habit of calling Mrs. Sandiland's place of residence 'home'—to ask if I would take my work and go with her to sit on the brow of the hill that overlooked the valley of Artois.

'It is "pig-killing day" in St. Pucelle, Hilda, and you will find it so much pleasanter to be out of the town than in it.'

'*Pig-killing day!*' I repeated. 'Tessie, what *do* you mean?'

'Only that each family here keeps a pig, and they kill them all on the same day. Also that they have an unpleasant custom of sacrificing the animals in front of their houses, and the poor things *do* squeak so.'

I threw all my writing materials to one side in a moment.

'Mercy on us! When do they begin? Let us get out of this as soon as possible, Tessie.'

She laughed heartily at my dismay.

'You need not be in such a terrible hurry, Hilda. I think you may give yourself a few minutes' grace. But it really does turn the street into such a slaughter-house, that everybody makes a point of going as far from home as possible.'

'Where is Ange?'

'She has gone up to see Mère Fromard, whose husband is worse this morning, and she promised to join us on the hill on her way back.'

'And your papa?'

'I left him in the *salle*. He is just going to start by the diligence for Artois. He has some business to transact at Rille to-day, with his friend Mr. Felton.'

'Excuse me for a moment then, Tessie. I want to speak to him before he goes.'

I flew downstairs as I spoke, and came upon Mr. Lovett in the *salle*, carefully brushing his clerical hat before putting it on. I had a motive for my haste. As we postpone visiting the dentist day after day, and then, in a sudden fit of courage, rush off without deliberation, and have our tooth extracted before we have had time to repent, so had I delayed speaking to my trustee on a matter of importance, and knew that unless I took my dilemma, like a bull, by the horns, I should never be brave enough to extricate myself from it. This dilemma was the want of money. I had been in St. Pucelle now for a couple of months, and Mr. Lovett had never mentioned the subject to me. I had gone there on the understanding that fifty pounds of my little income was to be annually refunded me for pocket expenses, and I had arrived there almost penniless, for the necessary outlay connected with the breaking-up of my home and travelling to Belgium had absorbed nearly all the ready-money at my disposal. I had thrown out more than one hint, in the presence of Mr. Lovett, that a few francs would be acceptable to me, but they had had no effect, and I was now really in need of some trifles for my toilet.

Moreover, Ange would complete her eighteenth year in a week from that time, and I greatly desired to make her a little present on the occasion.

So I felt as desperate as a young woman can do who has no clean tuckers to put into her dresses, and has just discovered an alarming hole in the finger of her best pair of kid gloves.

Mr. Lovett looked up as I entered the *salle*, and saluted me with his bland, beautiful smile.

'Well, my dear Hilda, have you any commands for me in Rille? I am compelled to go there to-day, to transact some business with my good friend Mr. Felton; but I hope you will be able to make yourself very happy meanwhile, with your own occupations and the dear children's society.'

'Oh yes, Mr. Lovett; we shall be happy enough. We are just going to take our needlework to the brow of the hill, and stay there till all the pigs are killed.'

'A very wise decision,' he said, laughing softly, as he smoothed round the nap of his hat.

'But I wanted to speak to you first,' I stammered. 'I should be sorry to inconvenience you; but—but—I want frilling and such a lot of little things, Mr. Lovett; and—Mr. Warrington mentioned to me, you know, the arrangement you made with him about it, and—*could you let me have a little money, just to go on with?*'

The murder was out at last! I had made as much fuss over it as if I had been asking a favour, instead of demanding a right; but it was over—the tooth was out, and I breathed again.

What had Mr. Lovett to say in answer?

At first, for the merest moment, I fancied that a flush of surprise or displeasure passed over his handsome features; but, if so, it vanished as quickly as it appeared, leaving nothing behind but his own frank, benevolent expression.

'Certainly, my dear girl, certainly. Why did you not mention it to me before? I shall be exceedingly annoyed if you delay asking for it one day after it is due. Let me see! When *was* it due?'

'I am not sure. It depends entirely upon how you intend to pay it to me. I have only been here two months, you know, Mr. Lovett.'

'Ah! Just so. And I generally give my girls their allowance every quarter. Still, it makes no difference to me, my dear Hilda; and you can have your money just exactly when you like. How much do you require?'

'I will take anything you choose to give me, sir.'

'Tut, tut, tut!' he said, as though annoyed by my want of confidence; 'it must be as *you* choose, my dear—it must be as you choose. What was the annual sum fixed on by Mr. Warrington for your private expenses? One hundred pounds?'

'Oh no, sir. Fifty!'

'That's not enough,' replied my guardian, decidedly. 'No young lady can dress according to her station for fifty pounds a year. We must make it eighty.'

'You are too kind to me, Mr. Lovett; but I should be very sorry to think my living here put you to any expense.'

'Nonsense, my dear Hilda! I do not pretend to be a rich man; but I must become poorer than I am before I consent to take one *sou* more than is absolutely necessary from the child of my dear old chum,

Dick Marsh. So we will call the pin-money eighty pounds, my dear; and please to say no more about it. But I must not stay another minute, or I shall miss the diligence. Good-bye, and God bless you. How like you are to your father, to be sure! As you stand there, I could almost fancy it was dear old Dick come back and smiling at me.'

'How soon shall you be home again, Mr. Lovett?'

'Not till to-morrow morning, my child; but Tessie knows all about it. Good-bye, good-bye!' And, waving his stick at me, the benevolent old gentleman descended the steps and made his way down the road as quickly as he could.

I was very glad that he had decided to fix my private allowance at eighty pounds, for it raised his feelings of justice in my estimation. To tell truth, since I had been in St. Pucelle, I had more than once thought that a hundred a year was too much money to pay for my board and lodging, for my bedroom possessed the barest necessaries, and we—that is, I and the girls—lived with the greatest frugality. The mystery which hung about the meals I had not yet fathomed, although I had began sadly to suspect the cause of it. On some days the dinners provided continued to be luxurious in the extreme, though, as I have said before, I refused to partake of them; on others, we were all alike compelled to dine upon the most meagre fare. It was evident, therefore, that the means of provisioning the household were not always forthcoming, though that was no reason that I should pay for more than I consumed. I did not, therefore, consider that I laid myself under any special obligation to my guardian in consenting to his proposal, although I admired him for making it. Eighty pounds a year— twenty pounds every quarter—would be ample, not only to provide me with suitable clothing, but to leave a margin wherewith to indulge myself by making presents to my friends; and with the remainder of my income, Mr. Lovett would be fully indemnified for any extra expense I might prove in the household.

I returned to Tessie therefore quite satisfied with the result of my bravery. At the same time I wished that my guardian had given me a few francs in hand. But I felt certain he had only postponed it until he returned from Rille.

Under cover of this assurance, I talked openly to Tessie, as we walked together up the hill, of the interview that had taken place between her father and myself, and of the generous offer he had made me.

I was anxious to have her advice as to what would be the most suitable present I could purchase for Ange on her forthcoming birthday, for, in common with all her friends, I had learned to love the girl dearly, and was quite sure that nothing was to be found among the paltry little shops in St. Pucelle good enough for her acceptance.

'I should like to give her something *really* nice, Tessie; something that she wants very much. Do you know of anything? Never mind the price! I shall have much more money than I shall want for myself, and my greatest pleasure is in giving presents to those I care for. If you will decide what it shall be, I will ask Mrs. Carolus or Miss Markham to get it in Rille. I know they are going over there next week expressly to shop; and they will choose it probably quite as well as I should do myself.'

But Tessie, considering her love for her sister, was singularly indifferent on the subject. She coloured when I proposed it, as I thought with pleasure, but she gave me no help whatever.

'Ange's wants are so few,' she said, 'that I think it would be a pity to take much trouble about it, Hilda! She will be just as well pleased with a bunch of flowers from your hand as anything else. I, myself, intend to give her my new muslin apron, and I know she will say it is twice too good for her and refuse it half a dozen times before she accepts it.'

'Now, Tessie! you are provoking,' I replied. 'One does not always ask before making a present if the reception of it is necessary to the happiness of one's friend; but surely we can think of some trifle that Ange would like me to get for her, whether she can do without it or not. Shall I buy a pair of earrings to match her silver cross?'

'Oh no, Hilda; pray don't!' cried Tessie

in a voice of such feminine alarm that I burst out laughing.

'Why not? They would look very pretty in her little ears.'

'They would be far too expensive a present to make her! She would not like it, and neither would papa. We have never worn ornaments of any kind; and Ange would not have that silver cross, excepting tha: it was given to Madame Marmoret at her own confirmation, and she gave it to Ange when she was quite a little baby.'

'And so that old vixen Madame Marmoret may make the child a handsome present, and I am forbidden to do so,' I replied, half offended. 'I shall not consult you any more, Tessie, but buy her just what I please.'

Tessie looked grave, but she said nothing more, and we walked on for a few minutes in silence. Then she began again:

'I am sure Ange would rather have a

ribbon that you have already worn than the finest piece of jewellery that Rille could produce.'

But I clapped my hand over her mouth, and raced her up the hill till she was out of breath.

'And now if you dare to open your lips once more on that subject, I will push you all the way down again,' I said, laughing, and she was fain to laugh with me ; for I was determined to indulge myself by buying something both good and handsome, for my pretty Ange.

The conversation, however, simple as it was, seemed to have affected Tessie in no common degree. She was unusually silent as we sat side by side, diligently plying our needles, and she sighed more than once as she looked over the broad valley of Artois. Her mood was infectious. She made me thoughtful, too, and I began to muse over that grave in Norwood Cemetery, and the dear, dear face that lay beneath it.

'Tessie,' I said suddenly, 'can you remember your mother?'

'No, Hilda! She died when I was only a few years old, and Ange an infant in long-clothes.'

'You are happy not to be able to remember her. You must miss her so much the less.'

'Do you think so? Sometimes I fancy I must miss her more. I have never had the benefit of her guidance or counsel, you know, Hilda!'

'That is true; but your father has supplied her place. A man's advice is better than that of a woman, however good and clever she may be.'

'Yes, I suppose it is, in most things; and papa has been the best and kindest of parents to us. Yet, if mamma had lived, Hilda, she might—I have always heard she was so fond of him—she might——'

But here the supposition of what her mother might have done was lost, in consequence of Tessie bursting into a flood of tears.

Her sudden emotion both surprised and shocked me. I had never dreamt that the death of a mother whom she had lost so early could have dwelt upon her mind to such a degree as this, neither had I ever seen her give vent to such violent grief before. Had it been Ange I should not have been so much astonished, for the 'little maid' was romantic and easily moved to tears; but that Tessie, who had so calm and equable a disposition, should be so overcome was quite another thing.

I soothed her to the best of my ability, but the storm was as genuine as it was unaccountable to me, and some minutes elapsed before she was restored to anything like composure. I was just congratulating myself that it was over, and thanking Heaven that no one else had witnessed her weakness, when I perceived, to my annoyance, the gaunt figure of Mrs. Carolus climbing, by means of a stick, the steep and stony ascent in front of us.

'Here is Mrs. Carolus,' I said hastily. 'Do dry your eyes, Tessie, or the whole of St. Pucelle will be informed before to-morrow morning, that I brought you out here and beat you.'

She laughed hysterically at the idea, and rose to her feet.

'Let me go back a little way and meet Ange, Hilda! I shall recover myself in five minutes, if I am left alone; but Mrs. Carolus's intrusive curiosity would be sure to set me off again.'

'Go, by all manner of means,' I replied,

'and leave me, like a second St. George, to face the dragon! Only come back as soon as your eyes have regained their normal condition, or the saint will be found to have turned tail as usual, leaving his stockings, darning-thread and needle behind him.'

This I said because I had suffered many things at the hands of Mrs. Carolus and Miss Markham during the last two months, and was noted for running away as soon as I saw them coming. Tessie smiled sadly and nodded acquiescence as she turned to ascend the hill.

'Oh, Miss Marsh!' cried Mrs. Carolus, now within a few yards of me; 'what an awfully steep hill this is! I really thought at one time that I could neither go backward nor forward. And the loose stones cut one's boots to ribbons. If I hadn't brought Willie's stick with me, I should never have had the courage to mount it. Why has Miss Lovett walked off just as I arrived?'

'She has gone back a little way to meet her sister. Why do you attempt to ascend the hill where there is no path, Mrs. Carolus? Boys and girls can do it, perhaps, and goats, but not——'

'Not older people, like you and me,' said Mrs. Carolus, as she cast herself jauntily on the sward beside me. 'Ah! that's just what I told Sophy Markham the other day. She will pretend to be so *very* young, you know—ridiculous it is in a woman of her age—and came skipping down the stairs two or three at a time, and the consequence was she sprained her ankle. I said it served her right, and she was angry with me, of course; but I am used to that. Mr. Lovett has gone to Rille to-day, I find.'

'He has—but how did you hear it?'

'By a very natural means, my dear or

perhaps you will say, an unnatural one. Sophia Markham has gone with him.'

'*With him!* In the same diligence, you mean.'

'Well, she could hardly do other than that, considering there is but one. No, I do not mean in the same diligence, only: I mean what I said, she has gone with Mr. Lovett. She had no intention of it till she saw him on the steps of the hotel, and then she suddenly discovered she had something to do in Rille that could not possibly be delayed. Dear, dear! I am quite sick and tired of her devices.'

'She wanted to get out of St. Pucelle on "pig-killing day," I suppose, Mrs. Carolus. Tessie tells me all decent people leave the town to-day if they can. Do you not hear the far-off squeaks of the poor porkers as we sit here? It must be horrible to be in the midst of them.'

Mrs. Carolus grew quite testy over my frivolity.

'Nonsense, Miss Marsh! You must be trying to take advantage of my credulity. But if you think it delicate or proper that an unmarried lady should ask for, and accept, the chaperonage of one gentleman in order to run off and see another, I cannot view it in the same light.'

'Oh, there is another gentleman in the wind, is there! That is lucky for Miss Markham, for I really do not think it is of any use trying her chances with Mr. Lovett.'

'Of course there is another! That is the indelicate part of it. The young man I once mentioned to you, Miss Marsh, as having been rather taken with the pretty Miss Lovett, is staying in Rille just now, and the way in which that woman goes on with him is disgusting—positively disgusting. If you saw them together you'd really say she was ready to jump down his throat. And she is constantly writing to him, too.'

'Perhaps there is a mutual understanding between them,' I suggested.

'Dear me, no! she goes on in the same way with everybody. I am sure, the scenes that have taken place between her and that young Thrale are a perfect scandal, and enough to ruin the reputation of any house. I have blushed scarlet, and so has my Willie, only to hear the things she says to him.'

'She has never struck me as being particularly refined or reticent, either in her manners or conversation.'

'Oh, my dear! you have not heard half of it! She tells such stories, sometimes, as would make your hair stand on end. And doubtless a good deal more has reached Mrs. Thrale's ears than she chooses to acknowledge, and that is the reason of her letter to me.'

'Mrs. Thrale! What, Arthur Thrale's mother? Has she written to you?'

'Didn't I tell you? Why, that's the real reason Sophy has gone off to Rille. She is so afraid of the inquiries that may ensue. This morning, my dear, I received a letter from Mrs. Thrale, whom I've never seen in the course of my life, begging me to look after her son, whom she has heard is very intimate with my friends and myself, and whom she avers has lost any amount of money since he has been in St. Pucelle.'

'*How* has he lost it?' I demanded eagerly.

'Ah, that's the question! How has it gone? The lad is staying at the same hotel as we are, at the instigation of Miss Markham, who persuaded him to follow us here, but, excepting out of doors, Willie and I see very little of him. However, Sophy and he have been *always* together—morning, noon and night, uphill and downhill; and I, of course, have had no right to interfere. But one thing I *know*, and that is, that young Thrale has given her the most beautiful presents; and presents, Miss Marsh, are not bought for nothing.'

'No, indeed! But he must have been very extravagant to make his mother write of him as she has done.'

'She says he has lost or parted with hundreds of pounds since he has been in St. Pucelle, and entreats me to reason with him on his folly, and to persuade him, if possible, to return home to his parents. But I have no control over the young man's actions. And how can he have parted with his money except by spending it on that woman? He knows no one here but ourselves and Mr. Lovett, and, I think, that elegant-looking foreign baron who lives up in the forest. Sophia Markham would have tried to get up a flirtation with *him* also, if she could have managed to speak French well enough, but, notwithstanding her boasting, she is a poor hand at it if she has to say anything out of the common way.'

'It would have been of little use to her if she had been successful,' I said, smiling, 'for the Baron de Nesselrode is too poor to make presents to any one.'

'Her face, when I taxed her with ruining Arthur Thrale, was a perfect study, and I feel almost sure she has done more than take presents from him. She ran upstairs and put on her hat at once, and not a minute afterwards I heard she was going to Rille. To see the other one, of course, and try what she can do now with him. For it is only an excuse, saying she wants to buy something, my dear, for we had already planned to go over in a party to Rille, to-morrow morning.'

'Do you still intend to go, Mrs. Carolus?

and if so, will you execute a commission for me?' I asked.

'Certainly, Miss Marsh! Anything that I can do for you. What is it that you require?'

'Next Tuesday will be Ange's birthday, and I wish to give her a pair of silver earrings to match the cross she usually wears. I don't want to spare any expense, Mrs. Carolus. I should like them to be as good and pretty as herself.'

But there I stopped, remembering that Mr. Lovett would not be home before the morning, and doubtful whether I should have mentioned the earrings to Mrs. Carolus before I had the money to give her to pay for them.

'I will buy you, then, the handsomest and strongest that I can procure in Rille, Miss Marsh.'

'No, Mrs. Carolus! Please do not. I forgot, when I spoke just now, that I shall not have my allowance till after Mr. Lovett returns to-morrow.'

'Oh, indeed! He stays over the night, then. But that is no obstacle, Miss Marsh. I will purchase the earrings, and you can repay me at any time.'

'Thank you so much! You are very kind,' I answered; but as the Caroluses were rich people, and I felt certain of paying the money in a day or two, I did not feel the obligation to be a weighty one. But it entailed my having to listen for another half-hour, at least, to the scandal Mrs. Carolus chose to retail me, until, to my infinite relief, I spied Tessie and Ange coming over the hill to put an end to the conversation.

CHAPTER III.

THE SECRET.

THERE was something mysterious about Mr. Lovett's manner and behaviour after he returned from that visit to Rille, which I could not account for. In the first place he was in the very best and highest of spirits, and the most extravagant dinners appeared upon the table for two days in consequence, whilst he lavished more than his usual affection and caresses upon his daughters and myself. Then, there seemed to be preparations going on for some great event.

A peasant woman was hired to clean all the upper part of the house, and for forty-eight hours remained on her knees in an attitude of adoration, scrubbing vigorously at the boards whilst Madame Marmoret stood over her and shrieked that she was a pig and a fool not to work faster. A spare chamber that had possessed no furniture of its own except a bedstead, suddenly became habitable, by reason of articles being secretly abstracted from our rooms, to repair its deficiencies.

I know that I missed a chair, a side-table and a water-bottle and tumbler, but no cross-questioning of Madame Marmoret ever elicited the fact that she had had any hand in their removal.

The next thing that happened was that Tessie and Ange were taken into their father's confidence, and were evidently much gratified by what he told them. Tessie, who was always cheerful but seldom merry, went about the house singing like a bird, whilst she helped Madame Marmoret to starch and iron muslin curtains and draperies; and Ange, whose happy face I had never yet seen clouded, seemed bursting with the weight of some pleasant secret which she had the greatest difficulty in preventing her lips from disclosing. A dozen times a day she threw her arms around me, exclaiming:

'Oh, Hilda! I *am* so happy!'

But when I asked her why, her rosy mouth was resolutely closed, and she said I should know it all soon, and I must be patient and wait. So I was patient, concluding that Mr. Lovett had received some good news of a private nature, in which none but his daughters had any right to share. A remark or two dropped by Tessie, relative to a change and a stroke of good-fortune, confirmed me in this opinion. I thought that his visit to Rille might have led to an interview with some clerical grandee, and the result was, the prospect of leaving St. Pucelle for a living of greater value.

I could not tell why, but as I dwelt on this idea, it gave me pain. I had already learned to love the quaint little town and its surroundings, and the thought of new scenes and faces disquieted me.

Meanwhile, the silver earrings arrived. Mrs. Carolus had executed my commission with more taste than I had given her credit for, and the massive Normandy work of which they were composed was the handsomest thing of its kind I had ever seen. My only trouble was that I had not yet received the money wherewith to pay for them. Mr. Lovett had been so exceedingly kind and generous in his offer to me on the occasion of my speaking of my allowance, that I did not like to worry him on the subject again so soon, especially as his mind seemed full of more important matters. Besides, he would be likely to inquire for what I required the money, and find fault with me for spending too much upon his little maid.

The only resource left to me, therefore, was to tell the truth to Mrs. Carolus and ask her for a few days' grace, which I did by letter, as St. Pucelle was visited by a succession of showers about that time, and we were almost kept prisoners to the house.

At last Ange's birthday—her *jour de fête* as she called it—arrived, and the little maid completed her eighteenth year. I was waked early in the morning by a commotion of voices chattering in the Wallon *patois* beneath my window, and getting up to see what was the matter, my eyes encountered a score or two of grinning faces upturned to mine, the owners of which held large bouquets of flowers in their hands. But the disappointment visible as soon as I appeared proved it was not me for whom they had assembled.

'*Ce n'est pas la petite Ange!*' they said to one another, shaking their heads the while. In another minute the casement next to mine was thrown open, and I knew that Ange's sweet face was framed in it, by the roar of delight with which she was received. '*Bon jour, ma'm'sel!*' '*Bonheur, ma'm'sel!*' '*Que le bon Dieu te bénisse, petite Ange!*' resounded from every side, whilst the bunches of flowers were held up simultaneously, till they looked like a forest of blossom.

'I will be with you directly, dear friends, exclaimed Ange, in their own *patois;* and the next moment I saw her in the very midst of them, kissing the women, shaking hands with the men, and laughing and crying by turns, as she attempted to carry in her apron one half the flowers they had brought her.

One old woman went down on her knees in the middle of the road and kissed the child's feet.

'She saved my boy's life! He would have died if she had not helped to nurse him with me,' she said, with the tears running down her yellow, withered cheeks.

In her hands she held up a common wooden chaplet, black with dirt and age.

'See, *petite* Ange,' she continued, 'it is all I have to bring you. It is not much, but my poor daughter died with it in her hand, praying the good God to bless all His saints upon earth. And you are one of them; and this chaplet must surely bring a blessing upon you.'

Amidst the crowd I distinguished Mère Fromard, the woman who had addressed me by the Calvary during the first week of my sojourn in St. Pucelle.

'I would have brought the best offering of

them all,' ma'm'selle,' she said, 'but you know the reason that prevents me!'

Ange went up to her and touched her forehead with her lips.

'All will come right in time, Mère Fromard,' she answered cheerfully. 'Trust to God! And how is your husband this morning?'

The woman gave some ordinary reply, and moved away in the crowd; but the look she directed at Ange was a strange mixture of surprise, incredulity and despair.

'It is not *her* fault!' I heard her mutter, as she fell back to give place to some one else.

When we descended to the *salle* for breakfast, we found it transformed into a perfect bower of sweets. Flowers bloomed upon the mantelpiece, the buffet and the floor, whilst in the centre of the table was a magnificent nosegay of every coloured rose, which had come from the château for Mademoiselle

Ange, with the compliments of Monsieur le Baron. And amidst them all moved the little maid, flushed like the very heart of a rose herself, with unalloyed happiness beaming in her eyes and irradiating every feature of her expressive face.

'Oh, papa!' she exclaimed, when at last her excitement had somewhat subsided, and we persuaded her to sit down to her meal. 'I feel as if this day was to be the commencement of a new life for me!'

Our little offerings had already been presented and duly thanked for. Tessie's new muslin apron adorned her slender waist; at her right hand lay a book her father had bought for her in Rille, and my silver earrings flashed and sparkled in her ears.

To say that Ange was pleased with my thought of her is to say too little. She was a true woman, and delighted in the adornment of her beauty as she delighted in flowers and birds and children and all the other gifts of heaven. She had coloured to her very eyes with innocent pleasure when I first put the ornaments in her hand, and had stood for ten minutes before the glass, shaking and nodding her graceful little head, in order to see them sparkle.

Mr. Lovett, too, whose censure for extravagance I had feared, seemed almost as gratified as the child herself at the manner in which the dangling silver things became her, and thanked me more than once for giving her so handsome a present, though he never thought of asking me how I had been able to pay the sum they had cost. Tessie alone appeared to be annoyed at my disregarding her advice, and indifferent to her sister's joy in her new possessions. Was she jealous, I thought, because I was in a position to make Ange a more valuable gift than herself? Surely Tessie, with her sweet good-nature and noble heart, could never stoop to the indulgence of so mean a feeling as that? Yet she left me quite unable otherwise to account for her silence and grave looks whenever the silver earrings were brought beneath her notice.

The post only arrived once a day at St. Pucelle, and whilst we were in the middle of breakfast, Monsieur le Facteur, as Madame Marmoret politely designated him, rapped sharply with his knuckles on the window-shutter and delivered a letter to Ange through the open casement.

It was for Mr. Lovett, and evidently contained agreeable news, for as he read it he exclaimed: 'Look here, girls!' which made Tessie and Ange fly to peruse its contents over their father's shoulder, when all three faces beamed with pleasure and anticipation.

'On your birthday, too, Ange! This is

quite a coincidence,' said my guardian presently; 'and we must have a little fête in consequence. My dear Hilda, it is time I told you——'

'No, no, papa!' cried Ange, clapping her hand before his mouth. 'Don't tell her yet. Let it be a surprise. It will be such a tremendous one! and you will spoil it all if you say a word beforehand.'

'Don't make it too great a surprise, my little maid, or it may have a serious effect upon poor Hilda.'

'Oh, papa, how funny you are! As if anything *nice* could hurt one! And Tessie and I have agreed that this change is to be a very, *very* nice one indeed!'

'If it is the solution of the mystery that has occupied you all for the last few days,' I interposed, 'you need not be afraid of the *dénouement* proving fatal to me, for I have all but guessed it for myself.'

'What is it then, Hilda?' demanded Ange.

'First, it has something to do with a change in the establishment.'

'That is right!'

'And it grew out of your father's visit to Rille last week.'

'Right again! I believe Tessie has been telling you.'

'I have done no such thing!' retorted her sister, indignantly. 'Did we not promise papa to say nothing till it was certain?'

I can vouch for my knowledge being the result of my own sharpness only,' I said; 'so you must blame no one else, Ange!'

'Very well. What more has your sharpness discovered?'

'That there is a gentleman connected with this change.'

'She *does* know it!' ejaculated Ange, with a very suspicious expression of countenance.

'You must have overheard us talking of it, Hilda.'

'With my ear to the keyhole! No, Ange dear, that is not my usual method of gaining information. Well, then, for a final guess! This change will take you away from St. Pucelle.'

'Take *me* away, do you mean? or take us *all* away?'

'All, of course—bag and baggage—and give you a new home somewhere else.'

'Oh no; that's wrong!' said Ange, shaking her head determinately — '*quite* wrong!'

'What! Shall you stay in St. Pucelle?'

'Of course! Where else should we go? What would papa do without his living?'

'Oh, then I'm out altogether, and my other guesses go for nothing. The gentleman and the change that is connected with your father's visit to Rille remain unfathomable mysteries to me. I see I have been on a wrong tack.'

'I'm *so* glad!' cried Ange, clapping her hands. 'Now, as a punishment for daring to guess at all, you shall not hear a single word of the wonderful change until it actually takes place. Do you understand, Hilda?'

'Perfectly! and as it is your *jour de fête*, I suppose you are to be allowed to tyrannise over your betters with impunity. I only hope when the revelation comes, that it will not be so startling as to prevent my surviving it.'

Mr. Lovett had been laughing heartily all through this little episode. He seemed perfectly to enter into his daughters' delight at teasing me about their wonderful secret, at which Tessie proved to be as good as her sister; and I think it would have been difficult to find more cheerful faces in St. Pucelle than rose from our breakfast-table that morning.

Naturally I suffered a great deal during the remainder of that day from the hands of both my young friends. They were running about the house like busy bees all the morning, helping in the kitchen and the bedchambers ; but whenever they crossed my path, they seized the opportunity to taunt me with my ignorance concerning their secret.

I am sure, if bright-haired Ange regretted once during those few hours that she had vowed her lips should remain sealed until the revelation of the household mystery was close at hand, she must have regretted it fifty times ; but she made up for her self-imposed reticence by chattering without ceasing to Madame Marmoret in the Wallon dialect. That amiable individual appeared to accept the impending change with wonderful tranquillity, although it was certainly putting her to a great deal of extra trouble. I did, indeed, once overhear her grumbling that she hoped things might turn out as they expected: that, for her own part, she had lost hope altogether, and never anticipated any better lot than to end her days in the poorhouse.

I saw Tessie, on that occasion, leave the work on which she was engaged, and walking up to the cross-grained old servant, put her arms about her neck and beg her to be patient.

Why was Tessie always the comforter, I thought, when Madame Marmoret's ebullitions of temper had reached their culminating point? Ange, who was all love and pity for the poor, and whom Madame had reared from an infant—Ange, I should have imagined, would have been the readier of the two to soothe and console her.

But the little maid, notwithstanding her universal charity abroad, never seemed to realise that any one within the house could stand in need of consolation. They lived under the same roof as her father—that father whom she credited with being the best, most lovable, most honourable, and most holy creature upon earth: and what could they possibly want more?

I believe that is really the way in which innocent Ange thought of us all. I have heard her say that Tessie and she were sure to be married some day, because if men did not wish to marry them for their own sakes, they would do so for the glory of being able to call Mr. Lovett by the name of 'father.' And this without a shade of coquetry or self-consciousness, passing over the unclouded mirror of her lovely face.

The remainder of the *jour de fête* passed very quietly; but I could see, as the afternoon waned, that the portentous secret was growing too big to be held much longer in the 'durance vile' of silence. Even a visit from the Abbé Morteville (one of the pleasantest and most intellectual of our acquaintances), with a beautiful little statuette, which he had had sent all the way from Paris to place on Ange's mantelpiece, could not do more than engage her attention for the few minutes that it endured.

The dinner-table, which was not usually laid in the *salle* till six o'clock, was ready that day by five. A snow-white cloth adorned the board, whilst at the four corners were placed, alternately, bowls of whipped cream and custard, and dishes of ripe fruit and *gaufres*, made by Tessie's own hands. In the centre of the table bloomed the Baron's beautiful roses ; any one could see it was a *fête*-day, by the unusual grandeur of the preparations. The girls had not changed their black serge dresses—indeed, I knew by that time that they had no others to change ; and I often wondered on what they spent the allowance which their father had told me he paid them quarterly—but they wore white muslin aprons and kerchiefs; and Ange had a bunch of damask roses glowing in her bosom. I remember thinking, as I saw her slender figure darting from room to room that day, that I had never seen her look so charmingly youthful and pretty before.

At last the discordant voice of the cowhorn, by which the diligence usually heralded its approach from Artois, was heard winding along the valley.

'Papa, papa!' exclaimed Ange, all excitement, as she rushed about to get his hat and stick, 'do you not hear old François's horn? Run along quick, or you will be a great deal too late! You know how he always whips up his poor little mules, as soon as he has turned the corner of the road, to pretend they have been racing all the way from Artois!

And Madame has everything ready in the kitchen—only waiting to be dished up on your return. Such dear little ortolans, papa! Monsieur de Nesselrode sent them down this afternoon for you, with his compliments; and Madame has the most delicious secret way of dressing them you ever knew! But if you don't make haste——'

'And how am I to make haste, you little puss, if you cling to me after this fashion? Give me my stick and let me go! I shall be back again within the next ten minutes.'

'And *now* for the secret!' cried Ange, as she jumped upon my lap, and clasped her arms round my neck. '*Now*, Hilda, yóu must be told! It is coming very, very close, and in a few minutes you will know all.'

'What a portentous expression!' I said, laughing. 'It is like the *dénouement* of one of Mrs. Radcliffe's novels. I suppose I may conclude one thing, however, Ange, and that is, that the secret is coming in the diligence from Artois.'

'Yes, yes! it is!'

'And that it wears trousers!'

'Yes, yes! Hilda, you are very clever. You always guess right.'

'But *who* is this mysterious stranger, then? and why have you kept me in the dark about him so long?'

'Because we were not quite sure if it would come to pass,' said Tessie, in her soft voice; 'you see, Hilda, when papa went to Rille last week, he met a gentleman whom we——'

'Oh, Tessie! do let me tell her!' pleaded Ange, after which they continued to interrupt each other, much in this fashion: 'Yes, he met a gentleman who wanted to come here for a few months——'

'To shoot in the forest, you know——'

'Yes! to shoot or to fish or to do anything

he liked, but he couldn't get rooms in the hotel——'

'Well, he could have got rooms, Ange, but they were not so nice as he desired——'

'Anyway, papa asked him to come and stay with us—but he wouldn't hear of it——'

'Knowing that we are not rich, you understand, Hilda——'

'But he said if papa would let him board with us, he would come for three months certain——'

'And perhaps longer, as he may stay over the winter——'

'If he likes the shooting he will: and he is going to pay us such a lot of money——'

'Hush, Ange! I don't think papa would like you to tell that part of it.'

'Why not? He couldn't come here without he did pay—and papa would not have accepted his offer if it had been too much.'

'Certainly not! still I think it would be

fairer to him, as well as papa, to let that matter rest between themselves.'

'You are quite right, Tessie,' I interposed, 'and I would rather not hear any more about the financial part of the arrangement.'

'Of course it is a good thing for us any way, Hilda. You will understand that; and we hope it will be agreeable, too. That is why we have all looked so pleased the last few days.'

'It *must* be agreeable,' said Ange, with a heightened colour, 'because papa says it will. And we thought he wouldn't come till next week, until the letter arrived for papa this morning, and——'

'Hullo, hullo! Who is that taking my name in vain?' exclaimed Mr. Lovett, from the open doorway; and Ange leapt off my lap as if she had been shot, and we all three rose to our feet to receive the expected stranger. I saw Tessie move forward first, and heard her utter a few shy words of welcome, but Ange had to be dragged to the front by her father, before she could be induced to contribute her share to our hospitable greeting. Then Mr. Lovett mentioned my name as that of his adopted daughter, Hilda Marsh, and I left the vine-covered embrasure of the window in which I had hitherto concealed myself, to encounter—*Cave Charteris!*

CHAPTER IV.

THE DENOUEMENT.

I AM quite unable to remember what I said, or did, in the first shock of meeting him again. His presence in St. Pucelle was so utterly sudden and unexpected to me, that I should not have felt greater surprise if my dead mother had stood before me; and I do not think that, for the first few minutes, I at all believed or realised that I was face to face with the man who had embittered so large a portion of my life.

I suppose I said something, and held out

my hand to him, because he seized it eagerly, and appeared delighted at the recognition.

'*Hilda!* Miss Marsh! Is it possible! Who on earth would ever have dreamed of meeting you here?'

The astonishment of my friends at his evident knowledge of me, luckily prevented my having any occasion to answer his remark.

'My dear Mr. Charteris,' said Mr. Lovett, 'you have taken us all aback. Do you mean to tell me that you have met Hilda before?'

'Have I *not* met Hilda before?' he echoed, in the old joyous tone that sent a shiver through my heart. 'Ask her yourself if you don't believe me! Why, we were the very best of friends some few years ago, when I was an idle young fellow, loafing half my time away down at their pretty little place in Norwood. By the way, Miss Marsh, I hope that your mother is perfectly well.'

At this careless question, which told me so cruelly how little interest I and my affairs had held for him since our parting, I raised my eyes and looked in Cave Charteris's face. Something in their expression, I suppose, added to my black dress, revealed the truth to him, for though Tessie interposed with a quick '*Hush!*' it was almost drowned in his apology.

'I beg your pardon *so* much! I am afraid I have made a great mistake, but it is so long since we met, you see; and I have been out of the world lately, and the reach of news.'

'It is no matter,' I uttered faintly, as I turned to Mr. Lovett. The old man folded me in his arms as though I had really been his daughter.

'Hilda and I have had a mutual misfortune lately, Mr. Charteris,' he explained. 'She has lost the best of mothers, and I one whom, though I had never had the pleasure of meeting, I reckoned amongst the most valued of my friends. Hilda's father and myself were sworn chums in the old college days, and, after his lamented death, there was nothing to which I looked forward in the future with so much pleasure as the hope that I might meet and be of service to his widow and child. However, there is a Power above that disposes such things for us, and that is the reason that you find Hilda here, living in my house, and second only to my own daughters in my affection and esteem. Go, my dear!' he added kindly to me, 'and tell Madame that we are ready for our dinner! I will take Mr. Charteris meanwhile to his room, and when we meet again, I trust we shall all feel more at ease than we do at present.'

I was so grateful to my guardian for dismissing me at that moment, that I fled to the presence of Madame Marmoret as if she had been an angel of light instead of very much the reverse. Her sharp eyes detected my agitation in a moment.

'*Eh bien!*' she exclaimed, as she fixed those piercing black orbs upon my countenance. 'And if they *do* want their dinner, is that any reason you should be as white as a peeled turnip? Mamselle Ange has been the colour of a carrot all day, and now you have thought fit to do the other thing! What does it all mean? Young men were not so scarce with me, when *I* was a girl, that they caused such a commotion as all that comes to; and if this stranger is to set the whole house topsy-turvy, why, the sooner he goes back to wherever he came from, the better; that's what *I* say!'

'Oh, hush, Madame! He may hear you.'

'And what if he should?' she exclaimed, raising her voice from sheer obstinacy, until it reached every corner of the house. 'I say nothing I am ashamed of; but I don't judge people before I see them, as you foolish young creatures do! I take no one on trust. I want to see my money before I give over my goods; and so I say, let him that pays quickest be soonest served.'

Mr. Lovett had conducted Mr. Charteris upstairs by a more imposing route than that which led through the kitchen, although we seldom used it because it entailed going through the garden. But I was very glad he had adopted it this evening, since it permitted me to reach my own room without encountering them again. As I entered it I drew myself up firmly, and knew that I must be brave, at least for the next few hours. I dared not stay to think: the opportunity had not yet arrived for the indulgence of such a luxury.

All I had to do was to brace my nerves to

meet Cave Charteris in the careless forgetful spirit in which he had evidently met me, and to ignore for the time being that we had ever dreamt of becoming more to one another than we were that night. I admired the coolness with which he had stood the shock of meeting me; at that moment I could not believe that his affected nonchalance was *real*—and I would imitate it to the best of my ability. So, in a few minutes, I descended to the *salle* again, looking as much as possible like my usual self! I found the girls alone there, the gentlemen not having yet returned.

'What do you think of him?' asked Tessie eagerly, as I entered. 'Do you not find him very handsome and distinguished-looking? He appears a true Englishman to me, with his fair yellowish hair and those very blue eyes!'

'*Bah!*' exclaimed Madame Marmoret,

who had just brought in a dish of trout and laid it on the table. 'What is the good of an Englishman over another man, except that he has more money and is a greater fool, so that he parts with it easier.'

'You are not very complimentary, Madame,' said Ange. 'You seem to forget that we are English.'

'I wish I could, *petite* Ange! 'tis the worst part about you—except the want of money.'

'You are always talking about money, Madame. Monsieur l'Abbé would tell you, you should not think so much about it. I am sure we have as much as we require.'

'That is as it may be!' grumbled Madame, 'but other people have not as much as *they* require, perhaps—*voyez?* Mère Fromard could tell you a different story if you were to ask her.'

'Madame!' interposed Tessie, in a tone of

remonstrance, which sent the servant muttering out of the *salle*.

'You are a greedy old pig!' called out Ange playfully after her, but Tessie seemed to be afraid of what the pleasantry might lead to, for she drew the little maid to one side and bade her be silent.

When first we sat down to dinner, Cave Charteris appeared to be so much overcome by the news he had heard, as to be rendered almost silent. Every moment or so, I detected him glancing furtively at my mourning dress and pallid features, and he answered the questions addressed to him by Mr. Lovett in monosyllables. I suppose he felt sorry that he had wounded my feelings, and the occasion of his doing so had revived some remembrance of the many little kindnesses he had received at the hands of my dear mother when she had imagined she was showing an interest in the affairs of the man who was to become her son-in-law. However, under the influence of the good dinner that Madame had prepared for us, and the good wine which had suddenly made its appearance on the table—heaven alone knows from where, for these unusual luxuries had a habit of springing into existence with us as unexpectedly as if they had been shot up through a trap-door at a stage banquet—Mr. Charteris soon shook off his temporary embarrassment, and became the most talkative of the company. Of course he was informed of the importance of the day, and insisted upon our drinking the little maid's health with three times three. Strange to say, I joined in these birthday congratulations almost as readily as if nothing had occurred to disturb the tranquillity of the morning. If I were a little paler and more silent than usual, the Lovetts attributed it to the suddenness with which I had encountered my mother's friend, and Mr. Charteris had no notion that I had been otherwise since I had lost her.

When conversation had been restored amongst us, he addressed the greater part of his to myself, taking care, however, not to make the slightest allusion to the old days at Norwood.

'I should think that seeing me walk in here, Miss Marsh' (I perceived, with gratitude, that he had quite dropped his old familiar habit of calling me 'Hilda'), 'must have been almost as great a surprise to you as meeting you was to me. And it all came about by the most remarkable coincidence possible. Have you told Miss Marsh where you met me?' he added, turning to Mr. Lovett.

'I have not. I wish now that I had, but my girls there wanted to astonish her with the appearance of a young man (young men being a rarity in St. Pucelle), and kept your identity a dead secret until you stood upon the very threshold.'

'Ah! just so. Well, Miss Marsh, I had been staying in Paris for the last three months, and had promised my uncle, Sir John Stephenson, to visit his son at Rille before I returned home again.'

'Sir John Stephenson's son! What, Fred Stephenson?' I exclaimed, roused into interest.

'Yes; do you know them? By Jove! now you mention it, I remember Fred telling me he had crossed to Antwerp after the summer holidays with a Miss Marsh, who was going to Artois. And it never struck me for a moment that it could be you. How strangely things do turn out! Fancy! the very name itself not arousing my curiosity.'

'I see nothing strange in it. It is so many years since we met.'

'It is indeed. Let me see how many—four, five, six?'

'Five.'

'Five years ago. By Jove! so it is. I was a nice article at that time, I dare say; I hope you will find me improved now, Miss Marsh. However, to return to my story: it was not the first visit I had paid to Rille, for I was over there last autumn, when I had the pleasure of making the acquaintance of Mr. Lovett and his daughters.'

'On the occasion of the Bishop of Otaheite holding a confirmation there,' interposed Mr. Lovett, 'Tessie and Ange were both confirmed. They had not had an opportunity of being so before, as, when the last Protestant bishop visited Rille, Ange was too young and Tessie had the measles. Young Stephenson was confirmed too, if I remember rightly. A nice-looking lad with fair hair.'

'Yes, that is he! I am going to ask you

by-and-by, Mr. Lovett, if I may have him over here for a day's shooting. I promised him a holiday, and my coming to St. Pucelle sooner than I intended cut him out of it.'

'Certainly! We shall be delighted to see your cousin, or any friends of yours, Mr. Charteris.'

'Thanks, so much! Well, Miss Marsh, where was I?'

'I am not quite sure,' I answered slowly.

'You were going to tell us how it came to pass that you met papa again,' said Ange, blushing violently at the sound of her own voice.

I saw Cave Charteris's eyes rest on her admiringly, and the thought of what Mrs. Carolus had told me just flashed across my mind and made me turn a little more sick than I was before. Only for a moment, though; the next I knew that nothing could make any difference to the relations in which he and I now stood to one another. I am not a woman hard of belief, but where I have been once deceived, I never trust again. Cave Charteris's pleasant voice roused me from my reverie.

'Ah! just so. Thank you, Miss Lovett, for the reminder. Whatever else I may forget, you may rest assured I shall never forget the occasion of my first visit to Rille! Well, there I was stranded last week in one of my very worst humours—and when you have seen me in one of my very worst humours, I do not think you will ever wish for the pleasure again. I have a shocking bad temper, Miss Lovett!'

He said 'Miss Lovett,' but he meant Ange; and the little maid laughed softly to herself in answer. I am quite sure she did not believe him.

'I had given up my rooms in Paris, and

gone to Rille for a few days *en route* to my own "diggings." And there I received a letter to say that scarlet-fever had broken out at home, and I must not think of crossing till the doctor said it would be safe for me to do so.'

'Oh dear! how sad!' exclaimed Tessie, sympathetically.

She was our only spokeswoman.

'Very sad! isn't it? But it would be foolish of me to go, especially as they don't want me. Well, just as I was swearing at this—I beg your pardon, ladies, I mean just as I was reviling my ill-luck—in walks your good father there, to whom I confide my difficulty, telling him, at the same time, that if I can secure comfortable quarters at St. Pucelle, I think of taking up my abode there for a short time, in order to have some forest shooting. Now you can guess all the rest. Mr. Lovett, with his usual benevolence, offers me the shelter of his roof for as long as I can behave myself, and his friend the Baron de Nesselrode has kindly volunteered to be my guide through the Piron. What a number of accidents, all coming together, conduce to this pleasant meeting! Well, I suppose it *was* to be, Miss Marsh, and I, for one, have every reason to congratulate myself that it has occurred.'

I tried to say that it pleased me also, though the lie left my faltering tongue but tamely.

' You have an engagement with De Nesselrode to-morrow morning, I believe ?' remarked Mr. Lovett.

' Yes ; that is the reason of my sudden appearance here. He wrote me word that they have got up a boar-hunt in the forest for the day after to-morrow, and I was anxious to see what sort of a mount I could get in St. Pucelle. I do not wish to send to Rille or Brussels, unless it is absolutely necessary. Are there any horses to be hired about here?'

'None to be hired, but plenty to be bought.'

'It makes no difference to me; indeed, I would prefer to purchase if I can get a place to keep the animal in.'

'We have an excellent stable and cow-shed adjoining the house, which are both at your service, being, unfortunately for us, empty.'

'That is settled, then; and will suit me far better than the hiring system. If I remain here, as I hope to do, for a few months, I should not care to be riding a different animal every day.'

'And the horse you will purchase here will serve your purpose better than any town-bred animal. It takes a stout-hearted little beast, I can assure you, not to turn tail in forest-shooting. But here it seems bred in their bone. Even our sheep-dogs have wolf-blood in them, and will attack anything.'

' I anticipate any amount of pleasure in the forest,' said Mr. Charteris; 'and if your friend Monsieur de Nesselrode is half as courteous as his letters, I am sure we shall get on well together.'

' He is a thoroughbred gentleman,' replied my guardian; 'one of the *ancienne noblesse*, who are so fast dying out of France. He is expatriated for the present—the Château des Roses having been one of the shooting-boxes of the family—but when he comes into his own again, there will not be a finer courtier throughout the length and breadth of the land.'

'So Miss Markham has given me to understand. She has often mentioned the Baron de Nesselrode to me.'

'Oh! do you know Sophy Markham?' cried Ange, with a childish giggle.

Cave Charteris took her cue at once.

'Who *doesn't* know her?' he answered, laughing. 'She is ubiquitous, and appears to be an institution wherever I go. I have met her at Paris, in Italy, Switzerland and Germany; at Brussels and Rille, and now I find her settled in St. Pucelle. I begin to believe I am never to be rid of Miss Sophy Markham, and if I crossed to Dover tomorrow, I should expect to see her face hanging over the rails of the landing-stage to welcome me home.'

They all laughed heartily at that, and Tessie said slyly:

'Do you not admire her, then?'

'Come, come, my girl! no scandal,' interposed Mr. Lovett, quickly.

'Ah, papa! I forgot you were one of the followers in her train.'

'I am sure papa is no such thing,' said Ange, indignantly. '*She* follows papa, you mean!'

'Here, Charteris! let us get out of this,' exclaimed her father, rising from table. 'You see what you have to expect from putting your character in the hands of a couple of little scandalmongers like these. If you will not take any more wine for the present, we will stroll down the town and speak to Jacques Despard about the horses. I know he has several nice colts for sale, and if you are anything of a horseman, you may like the mettle of a young, untrained animal. De Nesselrode will be up here by-and-by, I have no doubt, when I shall have the pleasure of making you personally acquainted. Tessie, my dear, should the Baron arrive before I return, tell him to make himself *chez lui* till I come. Now, Charteris.'

And, with a bow that included us all three from the latter, and a nod from Mr. Lovett, the two gentlemen took their way down the street of St. Pucelle.

Oh, how I longed to go to bed and bury my bursting brain in the feather pillows; to find myself quite, *quite* alone in the friendly darkness, and with the key in my door turned against all intruders.

My head ached from repressed thought; my heart was sick and trembling; I felt really ill for want of giving vent to my emotion: yet, so strong are the influences of custom and society, that I dared not tell the girls I needed rest. On the contrary, I eagerly denied their assertion that the sudden appearance of Mr. Charteris had upset me, and disdained all need of the affectionate sympathy they tendered me in consequence.

'My dear children,' I said impatiently, 'I assure you you are mistaken. I am not half such a fool as I look. I confess it startled me to see Mr. Charteris walk into the room, because, for aught I knew to the contrary, the man might have been dead and buried by this time; but that fact alone will tell you that we could not have been very intimate friends in the olden days.'

'Still, I suppose you know *something* about him ?' persisted Ange.

'How do you mean "*something about him* ?"'

'Why, about his family, and so forth.'

'Indeed, I do not. I never paid a single visit to his family—I believe they are Northampton people !'

'Norfolk, I think,' put in Ange, timidly; 'at least he said so when we first saw him at Rille.'

'Oh, indeed ! then I dare say you know a great deal more about him than I do. The fact is, Tessie,' I continued, longing to have the explanation over once and for ever, 'Mr. Charteris was introduced to us, many years ago, by an old friend of my dear mother's. He was hanging about town then, doing nothing, I fancy—any way, he used often to run down to Norwood to see us, as you have heard him say, and—and—we were rather intimate for a few months—that is, until his father sent him to travel on the Continent, since which I have heard nothing of him until we met to-day.'

'You knew none of his sisters or brothers, then—nor his parents?'

'I knew none of the family but himself. I think he used to speak to me of his sisters, but I forget how many there were.'

'He has only one sister now,' said Ange, again. 'I wonder if it is she who has the scarlet fever.'

'Most likely! Have you heard what profession he is in?'

THE DENOUEMENT.

'I do not think he has any,' replied Tessie. 'He seems to be a man of independent property! Did you hear him say that it made no difference to him if he bought a horse or hired one.'

'Yes; I suppose, then, he must have come into some money. He was not rich when we knew him. I remember that! He was to have read for the law, and my dear mother used to say—she said, I remember—I can recall her saying——' But no! put it which way I would, that sentence utterly refused to come to the birth. I had harped, unwittingly, on a string too nearly connected with my dead hope, and the discovery broke me down. 'Oh, mother! mother!' I cried aloud, as I put my head in Tessie's lap and sobbed without restraint. Of course they attributed it to the associations which the presence of their guest had recalled to my mind, and they were as tender and sympathetic with my distress as though they had been to blame for it.

'I am so sorry we kept it a secret from you, dear Hilda,' they exclaimed simultaneously; 'it was such a silly thing to do: but we had not the slightest conception that you had met him before, and under such happier circumstances. Do forgive us, Hilda! You will make us so very miserable if we think we have made you so.'

I assured them solemnly, as I rose and dried my eyes, that the girlish trick they had played upon me had nothing to do with my present state of mind. I should have felt the rencontre just as much I said, and truly, had I been prepared for it weeks beforehand; and I only required a few hours by myself to subdue the unusual emotion which old memories had raised in me. My answer had just the effect I desired.

'Do go to bed, then, dear Hilda,' urged

Tessie, 'and sleep off the remembrance of this unhappy evening. I am sure you will like Mr. Charteris very much when you come to speak to him more freely, and perhaps, in a few days, you will congratulate yourself that you have met him again.'

How little I thought, as I dragged myself up to my room, that her surmise would prove true.

CHAPTER V.

CURED.

THE chief feeling that I experienced when I came to review the events of that evening, was, that my unexpected encounter with Cave Charteris seemed to have dragged my mother out of her grave again. Until that moment I had believed that, little by little, I was learning to bear my great loss with hope and patience, if not with cheerful resignation. I had begun to think of my darling as in another and better world than this—if not actually in heaven, at least amongst the redeemed, willing to wait the moment of her perfection, and entirely separated from all earthly pain and trouble.

I had commenced to lose sense of the waking nightmare that had haunted me for so many weeks after her funeral; of the sight of the dead pinched face under the shrouding sheet; the waxen hands folded stiffly on her sunken breast; and over it all those horrid heavy clods of clay, the rattle of which upon her coffin lid would echo in my heart, I verily believed, until they fell upon my own. I felt the loss of her counsel, her companionship, and her love as keenly—perhaps more keenly than when I had been first deprived of them; but I thought that time had cured me of the terrible human anguish with which I had laid her in the grave. But now it was all revived. The sight of Cave Charteris had brought it back again; brought back the memory of her maternal interest in him, her confidence in his affection for me, and her self-reproach when we discovered that his attentions meant nothing, that she had not better guarded her one ewe lamb from the deceitfulness of the world.

I sat down in my room, and tried to disentangle my thoughts from my present position and cast them back to that period when Mr. Charteris had been so intimate with us at Norwood, and to see if my riper judgment could acquit him of having wantonly played with my affections. But I remembered it all too plainly, and I could find no excuse for his behaviour. He had not had the plea of extreme youth to exonerate his want of thought. He was five-and-twenty, and I nineteen. He must have known in what light his persistent intimacy would have been accepted by my mother and myself. Besides, though he had never mentioned the subject of marriage, he had told me, over and over again, that he loved me, and hinted in every possible way at the probability of a future spent together.

It was the old story—he had loved and ridden away; and, for many months after his defection, I had sincerely believed my grief to be incurable. I was very young and innocent at that period, and credited my darling mother with cold-heartedness when she told me that a woman might love more than once in a life-time, and better the second time than the first. I had been reared close to her side, and knew nothing of the wickedness of the world nor the elasticity of the human heart. I was one of those girls who believe that it is impossible for a married woman to flirt, or an engaged woman to break her word, without being branded with public scorn; and a great deal of my grief for Cave Charteris's desertion was due to the humiliating idea that my neighbours had observed his attentions, and considered me degraded by the loss of them.

This sort of unworldly ignorance did not long continue. I was not stupid, and as my girlhood merged into womanhood, my eyes became opened to the depravity of the human race; and I learned to despise Cave Charteris instead of myself, and to see that he had been utterly unworthy of the affection and admiration I had lavished upon him.

Yet the romance of my first disappointment continued to haunt and vex me, long after common sense had bid me rejoice at the escape I had had from marrying a man who was false as well as fickle.

It may be remembered how difficult a task I found it to tell the history of my heart to poor dear Charlie Sandilands, when he came to see me at Norwood, on the day after my mother's funeral. It was the false sentiment that still hung about Cave Charteris's hair and eyes and voice, that made the task so difficult. I would not have taken the man back to my affections at that moment, if he had crawled to my feet to sue for forgiveness, because I knew him to have been utterly heartless with regard to me—yet I could have cried over a letter from him, or a lock of his hair, or an old glove that he had worn, simply because they reminded me of the faith which I had cherished and lost.

Women and men are very different in this respect. Where a man's trust has been betrayed, he becomes hard and bitter, and thrusts from him, as far as possible, everything likely to bring the loss which he has sustained to his mind again. A woman may be as disinclined to pardon as himself—as determined never again to be deceived, but she cannot give up, all at once, every little tender memory that made her dead life so much brighter than her living one. She takes the ring off her finger—the hair from her locket--but she does not throw them away. They are like the dead to her. They have no more part in her existence, but they are sacred, and she covers them up with tears and prayers, as we strew rue and rosemary upon our corpses.

So, long after my own sense of what was good and true had condemned my weakness in shedding one tear for Cave Charteris, the beauty and animation and charm of manner which had first enthralled me continued to exercise their baneful influence over my mind. I had seen that beauty again to-day and heard that voice, and what did I think of them, looking and hearing with eyes and ears that had been healed of love's sickness? Well! he was very handsome, very handsome indeed; there was no doubt of that! I remembered having heard it said, in olden days, that he had been painted by one of the

Royal Academicians as 'Jason, and having been very anxious to see the picture for which he stood.

I could well imagine that he had made an excellent model for 'Jason.' He was tall, but not too tall : men over six feet in height are seldom well proportioned. His characteristics were strictly Saxon. He had yellowish hair, cropped close to his head in soldier fashion : china blue eyes—not large, but very keen and piercing : a ruddy complexion, and finely-shaped nose and mouth. The worst fault in his appearance was the light colour of his eyebrows and lashes : and the worst fault in his expression was a look of animalism, which I seemed never to have noticed until I sat down in my own chamber and taxed my mental vision to view my old lover by the light of the new eyes with which I had regarded him that evening.

It was not only because I remembered his behaviour to myself that the expression of his face had seemed cruel to me, as he chattered so affably across the dinner-table. Five years' self-indulgence had doubtless strengthened the outward signs of his inward character; but whether he had borne those signs in embryo when we were first acquainted, I could not then recall. If he had done so, I was probably too innocent to have interpreted them aright. But there was no mistake about them now.

I was considered to be an excellent judge of character, and I had examined Cave Charteris that evening as if he had been a perfect stranger to me; and read but too plainly, in the formation of his head and features, that though he might be as beautiful as the Adonis, his intellect was held in subjugation to his passions, and hatred or revenge would have the power to turn him from a polished man of the world into a brute.

As I came to this conclusion, deliberately and without the least rancour in my mind against him, I called out aloud, '*Thank God!*' for I felt that I was healed. As the poor diseased and dying creatures whom we read of in the Holy Scriptures touched the hem of the King's garment, and experienced an immediate cure, so, in one moment, the conviction dawned upon me that what I had been fearing was a mere 'bogey,' raised by the shock of Mr. Charteris's sudden appearance amongst us; and, save for a slight feeling of shame that I should have troubled my head about him for so long, I should be able to meet him on the following morning with an outstretched hand and a heart full of gratitude for my deliverance.

Tessie had suggested, as I parted with her, that in a few days I might congratulate myself on having met him again. But a few hours had elapsed since then, and I was already full of self-congratulations. For, had I *not* encountered him, I might have gone on nursing my sickly sentimental memory of the past, until the grave swallowed me and it together.

I felt such a sudden transition from the melancholy despondency with which I had entered my chamber, to a state of freedom and whole-heartedness, that I could almost have passed to the opposite extreme, and sung, in the gratitude of my spirit. I was like a person who has burthened himself for half his life with carrying about a heavy bundle that nearly weighs him to the ground, but which he considers it imperative, on account of its value, not to part with; but who, unexpectedly discovering it is composed of worthless rubbish, casts it from his shoulders. How light and airy he must feel!

How light and airy *I* felt when I saw my bundle of rubbish at my feet!

My dearest mother was no longer under the sod then. She had risen again to paradise, and taken the place my love had assigned her amongst angels like herself.

I threw myself on my knees beside my bed, and prayed to her more than to Heaven, begging her to look down and see how earnest and sincere I was in saying I was cured, and had no regret on earth, excepting that *she* was not there to rejoice with me.

I was so excited at my discovery, that I could not sleep until I had seen the girls again, and disimbued their minds of the idea that I was fretting in my solitude.

I opened my door, and looked down the corridor. The light was streaming in a thin line of silver beneath theirs. I stepped across, and entered gently. Tessie was already in bed and half-asleep; but Ange was leaning in her nightdress on the window-sill, with her pretty bare feet upon the uncarpeted floor.

'Ange! Ange!' I exclaimed, 'you careless child! you will catch your death of cold some day, if you are not more prudent.'

'Is that Hilda?' asked Tessie, rousing herself at the sound of my voice. 'Ange, why are you not in bed yet? It must be an hour since we came upstairs. And as for you, Hilda, I hoped you were fast asleep.'

The little maid coloured up at being detected dreaming in the moonlight, and jumped lightly into bed; whilst I approached to her sister's side.

'No, Tessie dear, I have not been to sleep; but I am all right again now, and I thought I would like to come and tell you so.'

'Oh, I am very glad, Hilda! Ange and I have been very unhappy about you.'

'I know you were; but it has all passed

away. Mr. Charteris's presence recalled my dear mother, and the days when she was with us, so powerfully to my mind, that I felt quite paralysed at seeing him; but that kind of thing cannot last, you know. I have taken the woman's universal remedy—'a good cry,' and my brain and heart are cleared by it. I hope Mr. Charteris did not notice my manner; but he will find it quite different to-morrow morning.'

'I don't think he did,' replied Tessie; 'we talked a good deal of you when papa and he came back again—until the Baron arrived, in fact. Mr. Charteris does not seem to remember much about the time when he knew you before; but he thought it quite natural that the sight of him should bring the remembrance of your mother back to you.'

'Did he get his horse?' I asked cheerfully.

'He has hired one for to-morrow, and

Jacques Despard is going to get a lot of colts up from the valley for him to see and choose from. And only fancy, Hilda, when Arthur Thrale heard of the boar-hunt to-morrow, he would insist upon accompanying them! and the Baron says he cannot ride a bit, and is sure to be thrown. Don't you think they ought to prevent his going?'

'How can they prevent it?' exclaimed Ange, 'the Piron is open to everybody. And Mr. Charteris said it would do Arthur Thrale good to be thrown, and take some of his "*sheek*" out of him. What is "*sheek*," Hilda?'

'Has Arthur Thrale been here again?' I said, too vexed to laugh at the little maid's pronunciation; for since Mrs. Carolus had told me of his mother's letter, I had had reason to suspect that some, at least, of the lad's money was lost at our house.

'Yes, he came in as usual. They have all

been as happy as possible, playing cards together,' replied Ange, with an air of complete innocence. 'I could hardly take my eyes off dear papa's face this evening. He did look so perfectly contented, sitting there with his friends! I think there must be very few people in this world who can "come down" as gracefully as he has—dear good old father! He, who has been used to a Court, and the society of the highest nobles and the greatest geniuses in the land, to be able to amuse himself in that way with one or two chance acquaintances! But it is all his goodness. He hardly ever complains. He is more like an angel than a man!'

This was the little maid's favourite assertion, and usually she expected no answer to it. But on this occasion the silence of Tessie and myself seemed to strike her unpleasantly, and she reiterated her words in the form of a question:

'Isn't he more like an angel than a man, Tessie?'

'Papa is certainly very good and contented,' replied her sister, but she sighed as she said it. 'I have often wondered that he does not more regret the scenes he has been accustomed to.'

'My wonder is that he ever left them,' I remarked. 'Why he left England in the first instance to bury himself abroad, and the Court of Prussia, where I understand he was such a prime favourite, in the second.'

'Because he is so good!' cried Ange, determinately.

'He had his own reasons for doing so, I have no doubt,' added Tessie, quietly, 'but he has never told them to us.'

'Well, I am surprised to think he can prefer St. Pucelle, and what one may call the "scratch" congregation he musters here, to the life he has been accustomed to. Cards and gossip must be sorry exchanges for the gaiety, intellect, and society that compose a Court circle. Besides, I hate cards.' I had made up my mind to say something more about the cards before long. 'They appear to me very uninteresting if played for love, and they are certainly very dangerous when played for money.'

'Do you think papa would do anything that is dangerous?' exclaimed Ange, firing up in a moment.

'Perhaps not, but what is safe for your father may be dangerous for others; such a boy as young Thrale, for instance.'

'Ah! if he went playing with anybody— yes! but that is just a part of papa's goodness. He will do what he does not care for himself, to oblige another person. I am sure Arthur Thrale's company is a great bore to him, but he will never tell him so, if he can keep him out of harm.'

'Oh, I see!' I replied, and said no more.

Ange took my words for what they seemed to be, but when I bent down to kiss Tessie's face, I found it wet with tears.

'If you think it wrong for young Thrale to come here, tell him of it,' she whispered, 'for I cannot.'

I did not answer her in words, but I kissed her a second time and squeezed her hand in acquiescence, and she understood what I meant. I did not intend to speak to Mr. Thrale, of whom I knew too little to be entitled to take any liberty with, but I thought that, if an opportunity occurred, I should be able to muster up courage to mention the subject to the Baron.

As I lay down that night, the thought of dear old Charlie Sandilands came into my head, and I felt so glad to think that I had not known the state of my heart when he asked me to be his wife. Because, if I had,

I might, in the lonely position in which he found me, have been tempted to resign all further trouble by accepting his offer. So many women have been drawn into marriage for want of money, or companionship, or protection. And I knew now, even better than I did then, that I never could have been even decently contented as Charlie Sandiland's wife.

CHAPTER VI.

TWO SERPENTS.

I DO not think that if Tessie and Ange had foreseen that the presence of Mr. Charteris under their father's roof was to entail a series of visits from Miss Sophy Markham, they would have rejoiced so greatly at the acquisition of their boarder. But she certainly lost no time in paying the preliminary one. As I descended to breakfast the following morning, I was surprised to hear her shrill voice from the *salle*, and stopped midway in my journey to demand of Madame Marmoret in the kitchen if it were possible that I heard aright.

Madame Marmoret, with her head tied up in a red handkerchief and gold earrings dangling from her ears, looked like a picturesque and pleased old gipsy.

'For certain it is she,' was her reply, 'and why not? *Ma foi!* one would think, to see your surprise, that eight o'clock was an unheard-of hour to get out of bed. It may be the custom in England, but for St. Pucelle, thanks to the Blessed Virgin and the good Abbé, who teaches us better, we do not waste the precious time here, when it is running on so fast to carry us to our graves.'

It was very strange to me that Madame Marmoret, who as a rule hated all the English visitors to St. Pucelle, was never heard to speak ill of Miss Sophia Markham, who was the most offensive of them all!

Was it possible she could imagine her old master would be so foolish as to think of taking a second wife from amongst the surplus female population of Great Britain; he whose habits and associations were so thoroughly naturalised to the country of his adoption, and who was too poor even to support his daughters and himself? Well, there were no limits to be put to the folly of men, young or old, in that respect; but I trusted from the bottom of my heart, for the girls' sakes, that it was not true. The mere supposition, though, made Miss Markham's voice sound more screechy and silly than usual, as I continued on my way to the *salle*. There she sat, in her walking things, a little apart from the table, evidently waiting till the meal should be concluded, to carry out the design that brought her there.

Mr. Charteris jumped up from his seat as soon as I appeared, all smiles, bustle, and animation, and set a chair for me in my own place.

I was so glad it should be so; that the remembrance of anything in our former intimacy that was likely to make us feel uncomfortable in the present seemed so completely to have escaped his memory, and left him free as myself to exchange the courtesies of a new acquaintanceship.

Of course my first duty was to say goodmorning to Miss Markham, which was returned apparently with much fervour. There had never been any open hostilities between this lady and myself. On the contrary, we were invariably most polite to one another; nevertheless there existed a secret feud between us, which, like a smouldering fire, only required the breath of opportunity to fan into a flame. She knew, although I had never said so, that I ridiculed her silly conceit, and despised her falsehood, and she never felt quite easy in consequence when in my presence.

On the morning in question, I disturbed her in the midst of an animated conversation with Mr. Charteris, which had set the cherries in her hat in violent commotion, which had not quite subsided when a shake from my hand made them begin bobbing again.

'Miss Marsh the latest of the party!' she commenced, with an affected giggle; 'why, I'm quite astonished! I thought you were the "goody-goody" one that always set an example for the rest!'

'I'm not aware that I have ever given the world of St. Pucelle reason to make such an assertion, Miss Markham,' I said, as I drew my chair to the breakfast-table and applied my attention to bread and butter and radishes.

'Well! I'm sure Mrs. Carolus thinks so, or she would not be so constantly seeking for your company. *I'm* not good enough for her, not half. She's so afraid I shall corrupt Willy. He! he! he! She says I have too many admirers to be a safe companion. Now, Mr. Charteris, *do* you think I've got too many admirers?'

'A great many too many, Miss Markham, for the peace of one!'

'He, he, he! Well, I can't help it if the men *will* come after me, can I? I can't get a little whip and whip them away! It was always the same ever since I was a little girl. I don't know what it is in me, but they *will* come!'

'It is very easy to see what it is that attracts them, Miss Markham,' said Charteris, with a side-glance at Ange that made the poor child choke over her *tartine.*

'Oh!' cried Miss Sophy, with a conscious look that went first down and then up, and was accompanied by a titter; 'you're too bad, Mr. Charteris! you really are! but you're just like the rest of them. That is what makes Mrs. Carolus so jealous of me! She will tease me to tell her what gentlemen say to me, and then—when I do—oh, goodness! She does give it to us—doesn't she, Tiddywinks?' to the yapping terrier which she carried as usual under her arm.

'You have to pay the penalty of being so fascinating,' remarked Charteris, who seemed to be the only one disposed to talk to her. 'Everybody knows what a terrible list of killed and wounded you leave behind you wherever you go. Look at poor young Thrale! You've "mashed" him entirely, as the young ladies in America say.'

'Mr. Charteris! How *can* you? What dreadful nonsense you are talking! As if Arthur Thrale could ever be anything to me but a friend!'

'I should think no one in their senses

could dream of imagining otherwise,' I interposed, rather too bluntly perhaps. 'Why, Arthur Thrale is not more than twenty, is he?'

'I'm sure I don't know what age he is,' replied Miss Sophy, rather crossly—the topic didn't please her—'I never ask gentlemen their ages, and it has nothing whatever to do with the point in question.'

'When had Love anything to do with Age?' said Mr. Charteris, still laughing at her, though she could not see it. 'Young as poor Thrale is, you know that you have made him your slave. Why do you suppose he intends to join the boar-hunt to-day, unless it be to hear his prowess sounded in your ears?'

'Don't you think it would be kinder to persuade him not to go, Mr. Charteris,' I observed, 'since I understand that his prowess is more likely to land him on the ground than anywhere else? He is an only son, you know, and if anything were to happen to him, it would doubtless cause great distress to his family.'

'Are you acquainted with the Thrales, Hilda?' asked Mr. Lovett, in surprise.

'No, sir, not personally; but Mrs. Carolus has received a letter from Mr. Thrale's mother in England, begging her to look after her son as much as possible whilst he is here, and she repeated the contents of it to me.'

At these words, two of our little party grew considerably rosier; one was Miss Sophia Markham, the other my reverend and saintly guardian.

'It strikes me as a very extraordinary proceeding,' ejaculated the lady, 'that Mrs. Carolus should go about St. Pucelle confiding the contents of her private letters to people who are almost strangers to her.'

'Most remarkable!' acquiesced Mr. Lovett;

'and I should have thought that had Mrs. Carolus required an adviser on the subject, the pastor of her church would have been the properest person for her to confide in.'

'Do you doubt my word, then?' I asked him quickly.

'Oh no, my dear Hilda! by no manner of means. If I am disposed to blame any one, it is Mrs. Carolus. Will you tell us what the rest of the letter contained?'

'No, sir; I would rather not. It was told me privately, if not as a secret; but if you will ask Mrs. Carolus herself, I have no doubt she will hand the epistle over to you.'

'Well, I never heard of such a thing before!' exclaimed Miss Markham, tossing her head; 'and it only convinces me of what I have known all along—that Mrs. Carolus is as mean as she is spiteful. She can repeat tales against other people, but she would be very much surprised if other people commenced to tell tales against her. I have held my tongue, of course, because I have made it a rule through life never to say a word against another woman's character, but I could tell stories, if I chose, that would shut every door in St. Pucelle against Mrs. Carolus to-morrow, and make the few hairs that poor old fool of a husband of hers still possesses stand on end with horror!'

'*I* never said she had repeated tales against any one,' I remarked quietly; 'but I conclude from your observations that you have read the letter yourself, Miss Markham.'

She coloured still deeper at this insinuation, but she was not to be caught by it. She was an old war-horse, and had been in battle too often to lose her vantage-ground so easily.

'No, I have not!' she said as stoutly as if she were speaking the truth. 'I receive too many letters of my own to have any time to spare for Mrs. Carolus's rubbish. But, knowing her as well as I do, I am perfectly aware that she is not likely to exchange ten minutes' conversation with any woman without trying to damage the reputation of another.'

I felt this conclusion to be so true that I had nothing to say in reply, and, the meal being ended, Mr. Lovett proposed they should walk towards the Château des Roses, where the meet for the boar-hunt was to take place.

'Are you really going to walk up the hill?' cried Miss Sophy, with sudden animation, as though the thought had never struck her before. 'Then I shall walk with you— that is,' with an arch look at Charteris, 'if you will consent to be troubled with a stupid thing like me. I love a brisk walk in the morning. There is nothing like it for health. I always go on principle; and as for Tiddy boy, he couldn't eat his dinner if he hadn't a run first. Could you, my Sweetikins?'

Sweetikins and Mr. Charteris and Mr. Lovett having simultaneously declared that there was nothing they would enjoy so much as the company of the fair Sophia, they all set off together to walk up the hill, whilst Tessie and Ange looked after them from the window with wistful eyes. I thought how they would have enjoyed to see the hunting-party start; how Tessie would have admired her Baron on horseback, and little Ange would have been pleased with everything; and I asked them why they had not also proposed to accompany their father.

'Oh no!' said Tessie, almost shrinking at the idea. 'Papa would have mentioned it if he had wished us to go. Besides, we have so many things to keep us at home. We are not idle people like Sophy Markham. Didn't she go on in a horrid manner with Mr. Charteris, Hilda, shaking her head at him in that absurd way? I felt so ashamed of her.'

'He doesn't like it; that's one comfort!' observed Ange, over her shoulder.

'No, I should hope he had better taste, or he would hardly be pleasant company for us,' I responded heartily.

I had done with him myself, but it would have been a step lower to take in humiliation, to have watched him in an earnest flirtation with such a battered heart as that of Miss Sophy Markham.

'I do not think Mr. Charteris is the sort of man that either of you will make a *friend* of; but the acquaintanceship even of one who brought Miss Markham in his train would not be calculated to render our home more comfortable.'

The girls both looked startled at my assertion.

'Not make a friend of, Hilda?' repeated Tessie; 'isn't he *nice*, then?'

'Very nice, dear, as far I know; but for friendship you want something more than "*niceness*." You want sympathy in taste and feeling; and I fancy Mr. Charteris is too much addicted to field-sports to make a good companion for women. Arthur Thrale is more fitted for such a capacity.'

'*Arthur Thrale!*' ejaculated Ange with glorious contempt, as she slipped away in answer to a loud demand for her in Madame's sweet voice.

'Hilda,' said Tessie, coming closer to my side, 'what was it that Arthur's mother wrote to Mrs. Carolus about? Was it—of—of—what we were speaking last night?'

'Not exactly, Tessie; but I much fear it has something to do with it. It concerned a loss of money on the boy's part.'

'Oh, what *shall* we do? what *shall* we do?'

I had never heard such a tone of despair in Tessie's quiet voice before, and when I turned to look at her the tears had gathered in her eyes again, and her face was drawn with anxiety and pain.

'Don't cry, Tessie,' I said, kissing her—'it is no fault of yours; and if boys will be foolish, they must pay the penalty. However, I mean to——'

'My dear Miss Lovett, I hope I am not interrupting you!' exclaimed the voice of Mrs. Carolus, at the open door; 'if so I will go back at once: indeed, I told my Willy I should not be absent more than ten minutes, but I just wanted to ask the question, have you seen Sophy Markham anywhere this morning?'

I had started forward to receive our visitor, and give Tessie time to dry her eyes, or the intelligence that she had been crying would have been communicated to the whole of St. Pucelle before sunset. I felt more kindly towards Mrs. Carolus also than to Miss Markham, because, although they were equally ill-natured to the world, the one had been more friendly to me than the other.

'Yes! Miss Markham has but just left us,' I replied. 'She was here before breakfast, and went up the hill directly afterwards with——'

'Not with Mr. Charteris?' exclaimed Mrs. Carolus, as she clasped her hands and sunk into a chair.

'Yes, with Mr. Charteris and Mr. Lovett!' I replied, unable to help laughing at the tragic attitude she had assumed.

'Oh, Miss Marsh, it is too bad! it is too bad of her altogether! I cast her off from to-day. I refuse to have anything more to do with her! She is not a respectable person to be associated with, nor to have living in one's house.'

'I think you are rather hard on her, Mrs. Carolus. She is very silly, I know, but you need have no fear that Mr. Charteris will do more than laugh at her! Indeed, I am afraid he was laughing at her all breakfast-time, but she did not seem to see it.'

'She never sees anything, my dear. She is eaten up with self-conceit, and if the whole world bowed down before her in mock homage she would take it for real, and accept it as her due. She fancies she is a giddy little butterfly, and that gentlemen admire her childish voice and ways, and are attracted by them. She would no more believe that they ridicule her afterwards than that they imagine her to be more than five-and-twenty! It is the *truth*, my dear girls. If I had to die the next moment, I should say the same thing. She actually had the audacity to tell me last week that Mr. Charteris had guessed her age at five-and-twenty. And she is five-and-fifty if she is a day!'

Tessie and I both laughed so immoderately at this, that we encouraged Mrs. Carolus to proceed with her complaints.

'When she came and told me that she had seen Mr. Charteris at Rille, and persuaded him to come to St Pucelle, I looked her in the face and said solemnly: "Sophia Markham, can you assure me that if that young man comes here you will not carry on with him in the disgraceful way you did last year at Brussels, because, if so," I said, "tell me at once, and I will leave the place before shame drives me from it." For if you could have seen, my dears, the things that went on between those two, you would have been as disgusted as I was.'

'Come, Mrs. Carolus!' I deprecated, 'you are taking away Mr. Charteris's character now, remember, as well as that of your friend.'

'Oh! my dear, it wasn't *his* fault! Poor fellow, what could he do with a woman running after him morning, noon, and night, and dodging him wherever he went? His life was a martyrdom to him. But where Sophia takes a fancy she has no mercy!'

'This becomes serious!' I replied, with mock gravity; 'what shall we do to save him?'

'Nothing will save him,' said Mrs. Carolus, seriously. 'Who is to control a woman of that age? I cannot do it! And fancy her having the forwardness to attack him the very first morning. She would have come round last night if she had dared. But, bless my soul! isn't that Sophy herself coming down the hill? So it is. The hunting-party must have started, then; she wouldn't leave them one moment sooner, you may take my word for that! Oh! she has caught my eye, I *must* nod to her. She has the most suspicious temper in the world, and would be sure to think, if she saw me here, that I had come up expressly to abuse her. Ah! now she must come in, of course, and I shall be obliged to walk through the town with her while she makes herself conspicuous at every step. Well, Sophy dear, have you enjoyed your walk?'

To hear these two women abuse each other when apart, and to see the marvellous transformation that took place in their speech, manner, and expression, as soon as they found themselves together again, was to witness one of the most curious phases of this world's deceit.

'Sophy dear' bent down and kissed Mrs. Carolus's cheek before she answered :

'Pretty well! I wish you had been with us, Lizzie! Monsieur de Nesselrode looked so graceful on horseback! and *your* flame Charteris has a seat like a centaur. I really think the horse Despard' has sent him would throw any ordinary rider.'

'*My* flame! You wretch!' cried the married lady, with girlish indignation, as she made a playful poke at Miss Sophy with her parasol. 'I wonder what my Willy would say, to hear you talk like that. And when I have just been telling Miss Marsh and Miss Lovett how you ran away from us before breakfast this morning, in order to see the gentlemen start!'

'I didn't do any such thing,' responded her friend. 'You are such lazy creatures, I should get no breakfast till ten o'clock if I waited for you. And it was really incumbent on me to be home again somewhat early this morning, Lizzie; for I must alter that new costume of yours before you wear it again. It is crooked in the back, and makes your nice straight figure look quite like that of an old woman.'

'Thanks, dear! You don't know what a clever creature this is, Miss Marsh! She makes all her own dresses and bonnets and mantles; and she has been so good-natured, since she has been staying with me, in altering and manufacturing my wardrobe, that I am sure I don't know what I shall do when she is gone.'

'Perhaps I don't mean to go,' said Miss Markham, facetiously.

'You droll creature! Not if some one of your numerous admirers proposes to carry you off?'

'Ah, that would be a different thing. But if I married to-day,' continued Miss Sophy, with the confidence in marriage of eighteen, 'you would send back for me to-morrow!'

'Did you ever hear such impudence!' cried Mrs. Carolus, appealing to us. 'She actually imagines I couldn't do without her! Well, Sophy, in that case, I suppose I should have to give house-room to *il caro sposo* as well.'

'I rather fancy you would! Do you think I should come without him? I shall make much too great a pet of my husband for that.'

'Well, he'll be a lucky fellow, whoever he is, when the day comes,' responded Mrs. Carolus.

Tessie and I, listening open-mouthed to this extraordinary example of feminine friendship, could not but believe that the last sentence at least was intended for sarcasm. But if so, no inflection of the speaker's voice betrayed it. The words left her lips as glibly as though she were sounding the praises of her dearest friend.

I turned away, sick at this exhibition of deceit, and thinking what mischief it was *not* in the power of such women to create, who could lie with impunity, not only to each other but themselves. I stood there, silent and thoughtful, until, to my relief, I heard their voices in chorus, declaring it was time to go.

'Good-bye, Miss Marsh! Good-bye, Miss Lovett! Come, Sophy dear,' said Mrs. Carolus, blithely.

'All right, Lizzie dear,' replied the other. 'Ta-ta, girls! I dare say I shall see you again before long;' and so they interlinked arms, and went down the road together lovingly.

Tessie and I turned and looked into each other's faces.

'Is it not sickening?' I asked her, after a pause.

'It frightens me,' she answered; and as I saw her pale face and lips, I believed that the insight she had experienced to falsehood had really caused her fear.

CHAPTER VII.

ALL FOR TESSIE.

It was about this time that my eyes became first opened to the fact that old Mr. Lovett, notwithstanding his benevolent aspect and many protestations of affection, was exceedingly selfish with regard to his daughters. How those girls worked for, waited on, and believed in him! From the making of his bed and the setting in order of his room, to the starching and ironing of his muslin bands and the cooking of his particular dainties, Tessie and Ange did everything for him with their own hands. And what was better, they did it cheerfully. There was never any question with them as to *which* should undertake the duties; they only vied with one another to perform them first. I never saw two daughters more devoted to their father in my life: yet there was a difference in the manner with which they served him.

Ange did it with blind unwavering faith in the privilege she enjoyed. It was impossible not to read her perfect admiration and pride in the expression of her face. Her father was the highest creature in the world to her, and she the most favoured of girls to be able to call him hers.

But with Tessie's service, willingly though it was rendered, there was mingled a sort of pitying fondness—more like the protecting love we accord to a child, proud though we may be of him, than the humility with which we wait upon our superior. I used to think

—and I thought a great deal in those days, more perhaps than was good for me—that the affection of Ange for her father resembled what a wife's should be for her husband (but so very seldom is); whilst Tessie's was more like that of a mother.

But without thus analysing their mainsprings, no doubt remained as to the love and duty they both displayed for him. And he took it all as his due. I could have forgiven him that, considering the relationship he bore to them, had he only appeared sometimes to consider them in return.

But his selfishness never permitted him to perceive that they made daily sacrifices on his account; that they lived on the commonest fare, pretending they liked it, whilst he enjoyed his flesh or fowl; and sat up late at night to recopy some faded old sermon, whilst he played cards with his friends in the *salle à manger*. Were he in the humour for it, he would keep them running up and down stairs on errands for him all day long, until they were quite faint with fatigue—especially Ange, who, notwithstanding her bright, fugitive colour, was, like most English girls reared on the Continent, anything but strong. And when he had kept them up long beyond their usual hour for rest, he would suddenly remember that a surplice, or a shirt, or something equally important, must be 'got up' by the following afternoon, and compel the poor children to be out of bed again the first thing in the morning, in order to get the washing and starching and ironing over before the more important duties of the day began.

Ange had said once that few people could 'come down' as gracefully as her father had. I used to think, on the contrary, that he had never learned how to 'come down' at all, but was like a spoilt child who will insist upon having all he wants, never mind what others may suffer in consequence!

His selfishness was especially apparent in the little trouble that he took to give his daughters any amusement. There were so few excitements in St. Pucelle; the days slipped away one after another in such a monotonous round of uneventfulness, that it was cruel to debar these girls of even one pleasure which they might have legitimately enjoyed.

Yet they might have been two little nuns, for the seclusion in which he kept them. Except to visit the poor or to walk in the fields, they scarcely ever left the house, and days sometimes elapsed without their putting their feet outside of it.

Their visit to the Château des Roses had been a real treat to them. They had talked of it for hours beforehand and for weeks after; but though the Baron de Nesselrode had begged Mr. Lovett over and over again to take us there for another day, he had put it off for his own business, until the matter had died away. On more than one occasion, during my residence in St. Pucelle, a little dance was got up by the visitors in the principal hotel, and the English curé's pretty daughters were asked each time to be present.

I had seen Ange's lovely face flush with anticipation, and Tessie's also, though in a less degree, but it had all come to nothing. Mr. Lovett had hummed and hawed and smiled sweetly on the inviter, and as good as promised his girls should attend the party, and then dropped the subject altogether. Once I ventured to ask Tessie why she did not remind her father of his promise, as he might, perhaps, have forgotten it; but she shook her head, and said it would be better not. Ange and she had no dresses fit to appear in, and papa would not like to see them worse clad than the rest.

'But a muslin dress, Tessie!' I urged, 'costs very little, and nothing could be more suitable for a dance in St. Pucelle!'

Still Tessie shook her head, and begged me to say no more about it, as it was impossible.

It was on that occasion, I remember, that I asked her, downright, what allowance her father gave her sister and herself for dress— and how they spent it.

'*Allowance!*' she repeated, with open eyes. 'Oh, Hilda! how can you think dear papa could afford to make us an allowance! You do not nearly understand how poor we are! Do you know, we should be unable to get on as well as we do, if it were not for the kindness of papa's old pupil, the Prince de Ritzburg. He often sends us a bank-note in his letters, and when we lived near the Court, and any English nobles or princes were staying there, papa was invited to the state dinners, and there was always a bank-note put under his plate. Wasn't it good of him? But he owes a great deal to papa, who was almost his only tutor.'

'But, Tessie!' I said, more interested in the question of her allowance than the gratitude of Prince Francius de Ritzburg, 'if you have no money who pays for your dresses?'

'We have only got a decent one apiece,' she answered, laughing. 'I think Madame paid for these; I know she went over to Artois in the spring and bought them, and grumbled terribly at the price. But they couldn't have cost much, Hilda; they are only serge.'

'I do not think anything you could wear could become you better, Tessie,' I said truthfully; 'still, I do wish your papa would let you go to this party. Ange *would* enjoy it so.'

'Of course she would—the darling! But we cannot afford it. It is quite impossible! so please say no more about it, Hilda.'

Yet the very same day, at dinner, Mr. Lovett had a dish of *salmi* of wild duck stewed in port wine placed before him, and I noticed that Madame drew the cork of his second bottle of Moselle before we left the table. It was such things that, little by little, let daylight in upon my mind, until it was enabled to read his whole character aright.

Monsieur de Nesselrode had been constantly at the house since the day we spent at the Château des Roses, but no one saw much of him except Mr. Lovett. He would salute us on entering the room, or passing in the road, and address a few polite inquiries respecting our health; but the strict etiquette which is preserved between the unmarried of both sexes, abroad, was in full force with Ange and Tessie, who never seemed to speak to a man except in monosyllables.

I confess this extreme decorum rather oppressed me. I was always longing to have my inferior mind drawn out and elevated by those superior to itself, and my dear mother had encouraged me in the idea that men were meant to be friends to women as well as lovers ; and that it was not always necessary that the last state should be worse than the first. I had been very proud, at one time, to be considered worthy of engaging in argument with such a clever man as Mr. Warrington, and had felt the greatest interest in trying to defeat him with his own weapons, which is not an unusual termination to such intellectual skirmishes. And now, to see Tessie's drawn-down lip and Ange's look of dismay, if I stopped to say more than '*Bon jour, monsieur*,' when we met Armand de Nesselrode, was aggravating to me. I wanted very much to speak to him about young Thrale, for I had an intuition that he would try and befriend the boy, but it was quite impossible that I should do so before Mr. Lovett or either of the girls.

I had determined, therefore, that when an opportunity occurred for me to see the Baron alone, I would set all the absurd rules of foreign etiquette at defiance, and tell him just what was in my mind. More than that, I do not mind confessing, at this date, that on several occasions, when I was able to leave the house by myself, I walked up and down the hill that led to the château in hopes of seeing him; but fate was against me, and we never met. It was to be, however, and at last it came to pass.

One day, about a fortnight after Mr.

Charteris had taken up his abode with us, most of which time he had spent at the château, or in the forest of Piron, some caprice—want of excitement, probably—took him back to Rille for a couple of nights.

We had been feasting—that is, I should say, Mr. Lovett had been feasting—more than usually well since his guest's arrival, and owing to that, I suppose, on the very day he left us the old gentleman was obliged to take to his bed with a bilious attack.

Of course, his girls were in a fine fright. If their father had been seized with *cholera morbus* they could scarcely have gone about with longer faces, and the fact that he could not eat anything seemed to fill them with greater alarm than anything else. In vain I assured them that fasting was the best thing possible under the circumstances; in vain did Madame Marmoret, who was in her very worst temper, thank the Blessed Virgin, in a voice that might have been heard at the other end of St. Pucelle, that her master at last knew what it was to have an empty stomach (though why that circumstance should render her so grateful I did not at that moment understand). Poor Tessie and Ange continued to look scared and pale, and could not be persuaded to leave their father's bedside even to eat their own meals.

It was a very lonely day for me, for I did not consider the duties of a ward included making a third attendant in the sick-room; and I could not help feeling just a little wickedly pleased, with spiteful Madame Marmoret, that my guardian's greedy selfishness should not go entirely unpunished.

'Mamselle Ange is calling you,' said Madame, in her curtest voice, as she thrust her head into the room where I was sitting, and ruminating on these things.

'Won't you do as well?' I answered, as

curtly as herself, for the woman's persistent rudeness was beginning to make me angry.

'You can go and ask her,' she said, as she slammed the door in my face, and I felt if this kind of thing went on much longer, I should be hung for putting arsenic in Madame's matutinal cup of coffee.

I walked out of the front door and through the garden-gate in the side wall to the corridor, rather than pass through her domains whilst she remained in so vile a mood.

'What is it you want of me, Ange?' I asked.

'Only to give a message to Monsieur le Baron, if he should call,' she whispered. 'Papa's kind regards, and he is too ill to see him to-night. Do you mind, Hilda dear? I would ask Madame, but she is in such a dreadful temper. Tessie and I have had to do everything for ourselves.'

'I don't mind at all. It is no trouble. But are you not coming down to tea?'

'I think we might, one at a time, as papa is asleep.'

I persuaded her to return with me, and, protected by each other's presence, we made a raid upon the larder, and procured all that was necessary for the meal ourselves, whilst Madame called us by every name she could possibly think of. We were 'pigs,' 'thieves,' 'beggars,' 'paupers,' 'vile English,' everything, in fact, that was bad; but we laughed in her face, and carried off our bread and butter and coffee to the *salle* in triumph.

And then I made pale little Ange refresh herself before returning to the side of her petulant old parent, when it was her sister's turn to come down and be comforted with the assurance that the attack would do her father all the good in the world, and bring him out again in the course of a few days with a more brilliant complexion than before.

They stayed with me as short a time as they could, and I did not press them to remain longer. I had made a great resolution to speak to the Baron about Arthur Thrale that very night. Such an opportunity as now presented itself might never occur again, and I was determined not to lose it.

So, after the girls had left me, I sat in the *salle* awaiting his arrival.

About eight o'clock he came. He looked rather startled as he perceived that, except for myself, the room was empty, but I soon told him the reason.

'Mr. Lovett is not well to-day, monsieur, and the girls are nursing him,' I said in my faltering French—I could speak the language better with any one than with the Baron—'but I have little doubt he will be downstairs again to-morrow.'

'In that case, mademoiselle,' he answered, 'I suppose I had better take my leave.'

I can see him now as he uttered those words with a slight tone of regret in his voice.

I was sitting in the broad window-sill, which was framed in a clustering wreath of vine and fig leaves, and he was standing leaning against the wall, and looking down upon me with those unfathomable dark eyes of his, and his broad-brimmed soft felt *sombrero* in his hand.

'Will you not rest yourself for a few minutes before you start again, monsieur? I said politely, waving my hand towards a chair.

'If I thought — if I believed,' he stammered—'that is, if I shall not be infringing the rules of etiquette, I shall be only too much pleased to exchange a few words with mademoiselle.'

'It is according to your own pleasure,' I answered. 'In our country, the rules are not so strict with regard to ladies and gentlemen conversing together as they are in yours. We have much greater freedom in England than you have here.'

'And much happier marriages in consequence,' he said, as he seated himself. 'Yes, I have heard as much, and there is scarcely a Frenchman who does not deplore the formalities of society that require him to marry a wife to whose mind he is a stranger.'

'Yet I suppose none of you are found brave enough to break through so formidable a barrier as custom,' I replied, curious to find out, on Tessie's account, if my companion were already *fiancé* or not. 'You yourself, monsieur, have doubtless been compelled to follow the example of those who have gone before you.'

'Ah! mademoiselle! I fear you are laughing at me. You forget the terrible reverse which my fortune has experienced. What father would promise the hand of his child to a beggar? It is true that I was *fiancé* to my cousin, Mademoiselle Blanche de Beaupré, before I lost my money, when our betrothal was at once cancelled.'

'You do not appear to have felt it much,' I said, smiling.

'Can I be expected to do so? I used to see my cousin at intervals in the presence of her parents. She was very charming—not strictly handsome, perhaps, but distinguished in appearance and innocent as a child. She would doubtless have been all I could have desired in the Baronne de Nesselrode, but I never spoke two words to her alone in my life.'

'Do you think she would have made you happy, then?'

'Ah! mademoiselle, happiness is hardly

the thing we think of most in married life. Society requires so much of us, it is impossible for a husband and wife to be always together; and to feel more than a proper esteem for one another would soon prove *ennuyante;* more than that, a source of unhappiness, because it would create a longing for each other's company which could not be gratified.'

'I cannot bear to hear you talk like that, monsieur. Marriage with us is meant to be the holiest and happiest state possible on earth—the fusing of two lives into one; and you speak of it as if it were only a matter of convenience, and a wife were an unpleasant necessity that the less you saw of the better.'

I spoke petulantly, for I thought if these were his real sentiments, what chance was there that he would ever cast his eyes in the direction of my modest, gentle Tessie, who, though not calculated, perhaps, to shine in the world of society, would make so sweet and true a companion for a man's privacy.

'Pardon,' he replied, 'I spoke of marriage as it is amongst us—not as it should be. But I confess to never having met with these perfect unions. I regard them as I do heaven, as something that may exist, but which I am never likely to see.'

'I have seen many of them. They are common enough in our country,' I answered, thinking of my mother's love for my dead father, and of dear Mrs. Sandilands, who had never changed her widow's cap and gown, although she had parted with her husband ten years before.

'So I have heard. In England people marry very early also, and on little money. That seems almost incredible to me.'

'Do you think, then, that money is the source of happiness, monsieur?'

'I have been led to believe that no *woman* can be happy without it. When a man loses his fortune, he loses all chance of being loved ; and that is a proof, is it not, that my belief is true ?'

'But I do not admit the truth of your assertion. A woman who is worth anything, will love a man all the more for his misfortunes. She is born to share and lighten his trouble. Whilst he is prosperous, he has friends all over the world. When he is unlucky, he should always be able to turn with confidence to the true heart that beats for him at home.'

'Ah! mademoiselle! you are speaking now, not of women, but of angels.'

'Then there are plenty of people on earth that ought to be in heaven!'

'We have not such women in this country,' said the Baron, musingly.

'There must be good and bad in all

countries, monsieur, if you only knew where to look for them. It is a common saying in ours, "A good daughter makes a good wife," and it is very true. To understand a woman's real character you must see her at home, with her parents and her brothers and sisters; and if she is loving and kind to them, she is pretty sure to be the same to you.'

I said this, intending it, of course, to direct his thoughts towards Tessie, but he did not seem to take the hint.

'You must have had an excellent mother, mademoiselle, to teach you like this,' was all he said.

'Ah! she was so good, monsieur! Had you known her, you would never have thought evil of any woman again for her sake. My father was once very rich, as you were, and he lost almost all his money too, through an unlucky speculation. We had to give up our grand house and carriage and horses, and come down to live in furnished apartments. The loss broke my father's heart, but I never once heard my mother complain. She never left his side until he died, and then she never left mine until she died herself. She was an angel to both of us; a true womanly angel, such as you may find in hundreds on this earth, if you have only the sense to know them when you see them, and the worth to deserve their love when you have found it.'

'I am not worthy! I shall never deserve such love!' he said, in a voice of pain.

'Ah! monsieur, forgive me for speaking so boldly, but how much worthier you might make yourself of it, if you tried. I hope you did not think me forward for asking you to stay here for a few minutes to-night, but I have a great wish to intercede with you—not for yourself, but another.'

'For Monsieur Charteris?' he exclaimed quickly.

'*Mr. Charteris!*' I echoed, somewhat scornfully. '*No!* If he chooses to do what is unwise, it is no concern of mine! He is quite old enough to look after himself. The one for whom I desire to ask your interference is young Arthur Thrale. He is only a boy, monsieur, and his relations at home are uneasy at the way in which he is going on in St. Pucelle. Will you try and prevent it? Will you speak to him yourself, and advise him to leave off coming here in the evening, and especially to give up playing cards? You know he loses money over them, and it is his father's money he is wasting, not his own! Even if it were, I should ask the same thing of you: to stretch out your hand and save him. I cannot do it myself, for various reasons, the chief being that I live in this house. Will you do it for me?'

'How can I tell the lad to give up that

which he knows I practise myself?' replied Monsieur de Nesselrode, with a very crestfallen air.

Should I be brave and go on and say all that was in my mind concerning him? His humble air reassured me. I resolved that I would.

'Monsieur,' I commenced again, pleadingly, 'give it up on your own account also. It has already caused the misfortune of your life, and the continuance of it must be putting the day of your deliverance further and further off.'

'It is,' he muttered in a low voice.

'Oh! monsieur! you have suffered very much! I know you have! Don't drive away the bright hope that is in the future for you—the double hope of being able to move in your own sphere in the position your ancestors assigned you, and of making a little heaven for yourself at home. Do give up gambling, for the sake of your friends if not for yourself: for the sake of those whom you lead into wrong with you, and for the sake of the future.'

To my intense surprise, the Baron leapt to his feet and seized my hand.

'I *will!*—I *will!*' he exclaimed fervently. 'As there is a God in heaven, mademoiselle, I swear to you I will never touch a card from this day again. You are right! you are *quite* right! Every word you have uttered sounded on my heart like an inspiration. I have been miserable for months past. Each day I have gone deeper and deeper into debt, and put, as you say, the day of my liberty further away from me. It may be years before I am free, but I will never touch a card again so long as I live.'

'Oh! I am so glad! I *am* so glad!' I cried, excited beyond measure at the unexpected success of my undertaking; 'and you will never regret it, monsieur! I am sure you will not! And Mr. Thrale, too! You will speak to him and point out the folly of his losing his money for a mere game, and give him all the good advice in your power.'

'Monsieur Lovett will be very much surprised at my determination,' said the Baron, suddenly struck with the difficulties that stood in the way of reformation.

'Tell him the truth! It is the best and most honourable course to pursue, and surely he can never so far deny his profession as to blame you for giving up what your conscience warns you against. And devote yourself to your hunting and shooting and reading, monsieur, until that happy time comes when you can go back to Paris and hold your own again. Perhaps you may marry Mademoiselle de Beaupré after all—who knows?'

'Never, mademoiselle! Neither she, nor any other Paris belle. Doubtless, when I am once more in the enjoyment of my fortune, many women — such women as I spoke of to you—will be ready to spend it for me, but it will be in vain. You have opened my eyes this evening to the fact that there are other women in this world—disinterested, whole-hearted and true—and if I can find such an one willing to share my poverty, I will work day and night till I place her in the position my wife should hold: if not — why I will do without a Baronne de Nesselrode at all.'

'Oh! you will find her, monsieur! never fear, if you will only keep a sharp look out,' I answered, laughing.

If he had told me outright that he meant to try his luck with Tessie, I should hardly have believed more firmly than I did that her sweet face was in his mind's eye as he spoke to me. It made me very glad. Her loving heart and patient endurance deserved so bright a lot that no one could envy her the best fortune that might occur. And *this* fortune, I felt as I looked at Armand de Nesselrode, would be very bright indeed. The young man had so much good in him, beneath the crust of despondency and defiance of public opinion which his self-entailed losses and the desertion of his relatives had caused him to assume, and I was sure that renewed prosperity and the love of a true heart would bring out the best points of his character instead of obliterating them.

To some people misfortune acts as a blister instead of a purge: it irritates instead of humbling them; and when the wheel turns in the right direction, gratitude makes them good. So I believed it would be—was already commencing to be—with Armand de Nesselrode; so I fervently hoped it might be, for Tessie's sake.

'Mademoiselle!' his soft voice broke in

upon my reverie, 'if I am not presumptuous in hoping you will listen to me, may I at some future day tell you of the chapter of accidents which led me to this downfall?'

'I shall be very pleased to hear it, monsieur!'

'I do not wish you to think me worse than I really am—you, who appear to believe I have still the capability of rising.'

'I *do* believe it!'

'Then I will try and make your belief a certainty,' he answered, as he bent over my hand and raised it, foreign fashion, to his lips, before he bowed and left me.

I was very much gratified with the success of my boldness. I felt that I had gained even more than I strove for. Monsieur de Nesselrode would not only give Arthur Thrale some sterling good advice, but do what was better still—set him the example of doing right.

ALL FOR TESSIE. 193

For what Mr. Charteris and my guardian might think of the new arrangement I cared little. They must play by themselves for the future. It was not likely I should interfere to save either of them.

But the Baron was quite different. The Baron had a great end in view which he was destroying by this fatal proclivity for gaming, and no means could have been too strong to adopt in order to rescue him. Particularly as it was all for Tessie!

As I sat in the evening light after he had left me, thinking of the interview just concluded, and softly stroking the hand he had raised to his lips, I kept on repeating, in a tone of the greatest satisfaction to myself, that I had done it all for Tessie.

CHAPTER VIII.

A REVELATION.

I HAD begun to be ashamed to meet Mrs. Carolus. Ange's silver earrings had only cost twenty-five francs, but I had not the wherewithal to pay for them, and I felt mean and shabby every time I saw her, and did not broach the subject of remuneration.

At last I resolved to make a second appeal to Mr. Lovett about my money. I did not feel timid this time; I felt angry. It was inconsiderate of the old man to leave me without funds for so long. It was part of the same selfishness which made him so unmindful of his daughters' feelings, but I was not his daughter, whatever he might call me before strangers, and I determined to put up with it no longer.

I am afraid I had not the ornament of a meek and quiet spirit. I never have had. I can endure a great deal when it is accompanied by an open and honest dislike, because we cannot always command our fancies in this world. But anything like shuffling, meanness, or deceit, has ever inspired me with the supremest contempt. So when Mr. Lovett, having recovered his bilious attack, was moving amongst us again. I seized the first occasion of finding myself alone with him to broach the subject.

'I think you must have forgotten my allowance, Mr. Lovett. I have been obliged to contract a debt in consequence, and am anxious to defray it.'

I did not speak very cordially, nor do I suppose I looked so. The things I had heard and seen lately were beginning to make me feel a species of dislike for my guardian. And his manner had not been as affectionate to me the last two days, either. Whether he suspected me of having had any hand in the Baron's determination not to play cards again—a determination which hitherto he had faithfully kept—I do not know, but more than once I had caught him looking at me in a suspicious manner, as if he thought me rather a dangerous animal than otherwise; and one or two observations he had let fall with respect to his dislike to see young women mix themselves up with affairs that did not concern them, rather confirmed me in the idea that more had come to his knowledge than I intended.

But that gave me little concern, and I spoke to him now as boldly as was my right to do, considering that I only asked for what was my own. He pretended to have forgotten all about it.

'Your allowance, my dear! Is it due?'

'I don't know, Mr. Lovett; but if not, will you please give me some in advance, as Mrs. Carolus, was kind enough to procure something for me in Rille, and I have not been able to repay her yet?'

He looked up at me, over the number of the *Siècle* he was perusing, with an air of great concern.

'I am very sorry to hear that, Hilda. To go in debt is to fall into an error which I have most carefully guarded my own children against. I would rather see them run about with bare feet than wear stockings and shoes for which they were unable to pay.'

'I dare say, sir, but I could not help it. I wanted something by a certain time—it was those earrings for Ange's birthday—and as you had not remembered to give me any money, and Mrs. Carolus offered to pay for them till you did, I thought it was no harm to let her do so.'

'Dear! dear! dear! This sort of reckless expenditure makes me feel very sad. It is a habit that will grow upon you, Hilda, and you must check it at once. And for my child's birthday, too; I should never have approved of your offering as I seemed to do had I known it was not paid for.'

'Well, sir, it was not my fault. I would have sent the money at once if I had had it to send. And, I assure you, you need not alarm yourself about my getting into debt; my mother and I contrived to live on our little income without owing a penny to any one. I am not a child, you must remember, first learning the use of money. I was my mother's housekeeper for years, and paid for everything we had. No one knows better than I do how to economise and make money go to its farthest extent.'

'I am very glad to hear it, my dear, for, unless you marry well, you will have to live a very frugal life,' he said, and he was actually returning to the study of his newspaper without another word.

I stood by him for a few minutes in silence, and then I began again :

'But I *must* have some money now, if you please, Mr. Lovett. I cannot put off paying Mrs. Carolus any longer.'

'Well, I suppose you must; but I do hope this is the last time I shall ever hear of your having run into debt, Hilda. It is a terrible habit for a young woman to get into. How much do you owe Mrs. Carolus?'

'Twenty-five francs for the earrings, but I want a lot of things for my own use, Mr. Lovett, which I really cannot go any longer without.'

'*Twenty-five francs!*' he repeated, as if those words were the only ones he had heard, 'that is a ruinous sum, surely, to expend on a birthday present!'

'Hardly so, for an ornament. I thought them wonderfully cheap. However, cheap or dear, they have to be paid for.'

'Twenty-five francs!' he ejaculated, for the second time. 'Why, it would keep a poor family for a week, and to think it should be wasted on a mere piece of vanity!'

'It is better than spending it on champagne or losing it at cards,' I answered wickedly.

Mr. Lovett flushed up to his handsome brow with anger. I could see the rosy colour mantling there, above the top of the *Siècle*, and I thought for a moment he was about to rebuke me for my impudence. But policy got the better of his annoyance, I suppose, for he elected to say nothing, at all events on that subject.

'You shall have the money this afternoon,' he observed coldly, after a pause ; ' I have no change in my pocket at this moment.'

' I shall have been here three months next week,' I said, ' so I suppose you will call that the quarter, will you not, Mr. Lovett ?'

But to this question he vouchsafed no reply.

'You said something, you know,' I continued, 'about making it eighty pounds a year instead of fifty ; but if that would be inconvenient to you just at present, I am quite willing to take what was first arranged between us — that is twelve pounds ten— at all events to go on with. You could make it up to me next quarter if you thought fit.'

'You shall have the money this afternoon,' repeated my guardian, in an offended tone,.

and leaving me quite uncertain whether he intended to accept my offer or not.

Finding I could get no further satisfaction I slipped out of the room, humming an air as I went. I would not let the old man see how vexed I was, but I remembered that Mr. Warrington had promised to make it a proviso that my actions were to be subjected to no control, and I determined that, if matters went on as they were doing now, I would take advantage of that clause and leave St. Pucelle.

Only for a moment, though—the next I felt that I could never separate myself from Tessie and Ange—and—and others there for such a trifle as an old man's temper. The hours passed away until the afternoon, when I had agreed to take a walk with Tessie ; and as I entered my room to dress, I spied a small round white packet, which decidedly held money, placed upon my toilet-table.

'Hurrah!' I mentallly ejaculated. 'It is all right, then! Here is my allowance.'

I quickly unfolded the coins. Inside their wrapper was written in pencil:

'My dear Hilda,

'I enclose you the means by which to defray your debt to Mrs. Carolus, and I sincerely trust it may be the last you will ever incur,

'Yours truly,

'Horace Lovett.'

I counted the money that lay upon the table. Twenty-five francs alone. The exact sum I owed for the earrings, and not a sou over to purchase any necessaries for myself.

It was too bad! I could have cried with vexation and disappointment. All the trouble I had taken had been thrown away, and it was evident that if I wished to get anything more out of the Reverend Horace, the unpleasant scenes I had passed through would have to be enacted over again. But I resolved it should not be so; that I would not subject myself to any further humiliation, but write straight to Mr. Warrington instead, and inform him of the state of affairs and ask him to settle matters with Mr. Lovett for me.

My face was still heated with excitement and annoyance, when Tessie knocked at my door and asked if I were ready to go out. I threw the coins into a drawer and joined her at once.

I was not in a mood to prove very pleasant company, but anything is better than staying at home to brood over trouble. The good influences to which we lay ourselves open, always make it appear less in the fresh air.

Tessie was an excellent sympathiser. She

knew when to talk and when to be silent, and on the present occasion she let me walk along in converse with myself only, until shame roused me to be more serviceable and friendly.

'Where is Ange, Tessie?'

'Lying down at home with a headache.'

'That is very unlike the "little maid," is it not?'

'Yes! Not that she exactly confessed to a headache; but she was lazy, and preferred reading one of the books Mr. Charteris brought from Rille the other day.'

'Ah! *c'est autre chose!* You look as if you had a headache too, Tessie.'

'Do I? I have been a little worried, that is all.'

'Poor child! which of us is without worries? Have we any particular end in walking this way?'

We were on the road to the Château des Roses.

'Yes, I want to call at the Fromards'. Guillaume is worse to-day, and—and papa has sent them a little money.'

' That is very good of him,' I remarked sarcastically, wishing that 'papa' would be just before he was generous.

We were scarcely prepared, however, for the scene that awaited us in the cottage of the Fromards. It was a poor place, with plastered walls and a deep thatched roof that almost extinguished it.

The sides of the house were yellow and green with dirt and decay, and the smoke of the peat fire was issuing from a hole in the roof, instead of by its legitimate egress, the dilapidated chimney. In front of the entrance door ran a gutter of filthy water, and a large heap of manure and refuse was banked up against the wooden stand which was to be seen outside each door in St. Pucelle, and on which the slaughtered pigs were laid out to be halved and quartered.

A few fowls regaling themselves on the dunghill recalled to my mind the fact that it was here Ange came whenever she wanted fresh eggs for her father's breakfast; but I had barely had time to take in the surroundings of the place, before we were saluted by a loud howl from the doorway, and the Mère Fromard rushed forward, and, seizing Tessie's hands, began explaining in her Wallon *patois* how her good Guillaume had gone to his rest but half an hour before, and she was left a lonely widow, with five poor children to battle for in this hard world alone.

Before we knew what was going to happen to us, we had been dragged into the presence of the defunct Guillaume, who already lay shrouded and stretched out on two planks in a corner of the general sitting-room, whilst his younger children played on the ground beside him, and one or two fowls, more inquisitive or hungry than the rest, were picking up the crumbs of potato that had fallen on the brick floor.

As we entered the house and her eye fell upon the corpse, I saw Tessie's face turn as white as death itself. Not knowing how far she was accustomed to such scenes, I wanted to draw her back again; but Madame Fromard insisted upon her going forward.

'Why should she not see him?' she exclaimed; 'she has watched him dying for months past; for the want of bread, mamselle, the bread it was his right to have had, and which would have saved him may be from the grave this day. And she was not afraid then—neither she nor Monsieur le Curé—and now that he is silent for ever—that he can no longer speak and ask for his own—why should she be afraid to look on his face, unless it be to remember how it has come to be so still and so silent?'

The woman seemed as if she had gone out of her senses, as she pushed us to the very feet of the corpse and snatched the covering from off its face.

'Look at him,' she said loudly, 'and remember that he died from want! Sixty—a hundred francs would have saved him, mamselle; and he was owed five hundred and fifty, but couldn't get it. Ah, Guillaume! husband of my youth! father of my children! thou art gone to the judgment-seat of God, to arrange a fearful reckoning for them that sent thee there so long before thy time.'

'Madame! madame!' said Tessie, who unaccountably to me had begun to sob in unison with Mère Fromard. 'Don't speak like that—pray don't! We have all felt for you so much, and papa sent you this in hopes it might be of use to poor Guillaume' (putting something timidly into the woman's hand); 'and he would have done more if he could; you know he would, madame.'

Mère Fromard unclasped her hand and displayed a five-franc piece, then, with sudden energy, sent it spinning to the other end of the brick floor.

'A five-franc piece!' she cried scornfully; 'a five franc-piece, when he owes him five hundred and fifty. Oh! it is no use to shake your head at me and cry, mamselle. The time is past for that! I have been very patient for a long, long time, but I didn't think it would end like this. I thought my poor Guillaume would have got up again to see after that which was his—all his little savings—all the *dot* I brought him at our marriage of two hundred francs—lent in an evil moment and never returned again—whilst he dies for want of proper warmth and nourishment.'

Madame Fromard had been running on in her usually (to me) incomprehensible dialect, but I gathered enough of her discourse to-day to be curious to learn more.

'*Who* has been so wicked as to defraud your family like this?' I asked.

'No! no! do not say it!' cried Tessie, vehemently, as she seized Mère Fromard's hand and kissed it.

But the woman flung hers away. She seemed to have changed to-day from a patient sufferer into a demon.

'I *will* say it!' she exclaimed. 'Are his evil deeds always to be covered up with excuses and promises and fair words. It is the Curé Anglais, mamselle,' she continued, turning to me. 'It is Monsieur Lovett who borrowed my poor Guillaume's savings, two, three, five years ago, and has been promising, promising, promising ever since to pay us back again, but never more than a few sous at a time. Who would have doubted him, mamselle, a man so good-intentioned, so benevolent, so charitable to the poor! We thought our money was safer than in a bank. We had lent it to the *Bon Dieu* to accommodate His servant. It was bound to come back with blessings upon us, and it has come with *that*,' she said pathetically, pointing to her dead husband, 'with a five-franc piece and a corpse! Bah! there can be no heaven, or such things would not be allowed.'

'Is this *possible?*' I said, in a tone of the greatest amazement. ' Tessie! she must have gone out of her mind. She cannot know what she is saying!'

But this insinuation only stimulated Madame Fromard to make her meaning plainer.

'*Possible!*' she screamed, 'is it possible that Monsieur le Curé owes money all over

St. Pucelle and Rille—that there is not a tradesman who has not his name down for a larger sum than he will ever pay whilst living, and that when he dies they will swoop down upon his carcass like birds of prey, to see which can tear it to pieces first! *Bon Dieu!* Mamselle is not so foolish as she would make herself to be! She *must* know that if it were not for the Prince Francius von Ritzburg, Monsieur le Curé would have been in prison years ago, and that it is only because of his holy profession he is allowed to walk free about the streets of St. Pucelle! But the day will come—the day will come when my poor Guillaume shall be avenged of his death!'

We could do the raving woman no good, and Tessie was crying so bitterly by this time, that I drew her quickly out of the cottage, and led her to a secluded part of the encircling country where she could sit down and weep in privacy. I did not know what to say to her. If this horrid story were untrue, why did she not deny it—why did she sit there with her face buried in her hands and cry as if her heart would break? And if it were *true*, as I too much feared it must be, what comfort could I give her? For I felt that I would rather have died myself than have heard such words spoken of *my* father, and been unable to refute them.

I sat by her side in silence, waiting until she should speak to me. The first words she said were confirmatory of my fears.

'Don't tell Ange of this—pray don't tell her, Hilda! She knows nothing of it all. It would break her heart!'

'It is true then, Tessie?'

She did not answer me except by another convulsive sob.

'I don't think it is all his fault,' she said presently; 'we have been so very poor, you see, and debts accumulate so fast, it seems impossible to gain ground again when once you have lost it. And I know that his liabilities have weighed heavily upon poor papa's mind, this one to poor Guillaume especially. We have always been friendly with them, and had our eggs of them for that reason, but what could papa do? Five hundred and fifty francs! it is a positive fortune. We shall never be able to pay it!'

'Meanwhile they starve,' I said bitterly.

'Oh, Hilda! don't be hard. You don't know how terribly I feel it. The Prince has been very kind to us, and sometimes I have thought I would beg my way to the Court and tell him all about it, and see if he would help us to pay off papa's debts.'

'It would be of no use, Tessie. When men have once got into the habit of debt and learned to look upon it with indifference, they are past cure. He would only start clear, to get into debt again.'

'I have always pitied him so,' continued Tessie, in a low voice, 'because he used to live in such different style, you know, with every comfort about him, and it must have been such a dreadful trial to come down to his present life. And I have thought, sometimes, that he had such a fresh innocent sort of mind, he really did not think how fast money went, nor what trouble he was laying up for himself and us in the future. Sometimes I hardly believe he realises it now. He seems so happy and contented and cheerful under it all.'

I could not say anything to her either in acquiescence or by way of consolation. I thought of the innocent ingenuous Harold Skimpole in 'Bleak House,' who cheated everybody, and was too childlike to understand what he was doing, and I felt nothing but contempt and disgust for my reverend guardian. I understood now the farce he had been playing with regard to my little allowance, and felt sure that unless some desperate effort were made on my behalf, I should never see any of it at all.

'You will not tell Ange?' reiterated Tessie, pleadingly.

'No, Tessie! certainly not, since you desire it. But do you think it possible she does not guess the state of affairs?'

'Oh, I am *sure* she does not. It would kill Ange to think papa one whit less perfect than she does. You don't know how she loves him, Hilda. Even Madame Marmoret, who is very spiteful sometimes against poor papa in my presence, has never mentioned a word about him to Ange, because she says she is sure she will never smile again if she once knows it.'

'I suppose your father owes Madame

Marmoret money also then, I said bluntly.

I was resolved, now I had ascertained so much, to hear the whole of it. It was best to see the extent of the danger which I ran.

'Yes,' replied Tessie, hesitatingly, 'and her wages must have fallen a long way behind also. Poor Madame has had much to try her, and I do not wonder that sometimes she feels a little sore and angry. Ange is not always so patient with her as she might be. She does not know the reason as I do.'

'Why does Madame dislike me so much, Tessie?'

'I don't think she dislikes you personally, but she thought your coming to live with us would be an extra expense and increase papa's debts, I suppose. She knows that the goodness of papa's heart often overbalances the greatness of his mind.'

'But is she not aware, then, that I pay

your father a hundred a year for my board and lodging?'

Tessie looked round at me with a face of astonishment.

'Hilda! is that so?' she demanded.

'Of course it is so! Have you not been told it before?'

'Never!'

'And what did you suppose, then? That I was living on your father's charity?'

'Oh, dear Hilda!' cried the girl, embracing me warmly. 'We should never have called it by a name like that! Ange and I thought that as you were the child of one of papa's dearest friends, it was the most natural thing in the world that when you were orphaned you should come to live with us and be our sister. We never asked if you had money or not. Our only anxiety was that you should love us.'

'It is true nevertheless, dear Tessie. My

noble income consists of one hundred and fifty pounds a year, and of that Mr. Lovett agreed with Mr. Warrington, my solicitor, to allow me fifty pounds for my private expenses, and to retain the remainder as payment for my board and lodging in St. Pucelle.'

'And—and—have you had your allowance, Hilda?' asked Tessie, anxiously.

'No, dear, I have not, I am sorry to say. After much persuasion, your father has given me twenty-five francs to repay Mrs. Carolus for Ange's earrings, but for the rest of my pocket-money I expect I may do what is vulgarly termed *whistle.*'

She flung herself in my arms in a fresh burst of tears.

'Oh, Hilda! don't love Ange and me less because of this. We have grown so fond of you. We feel just as if you were our sister. Don't turn against us—it isn't our fault, dear

—we would cut off our right hands to serve you if we could.'

I assured her again and again that I would never be less her friend and her sister's friend than I was at that moment.

'I love you too, Tessie—rest sure of that, and we will fight this great trouble out together if we can. I will not turn against you, nor will I forsake you. My lot has not been so unexpectedly cast here without some good reason, and I should feel like a coward if I could run away just as I have heard all, and leave you and Ange to cope with this misery by yourselves.'

'But remember, she knows nothing,' said Tessie, with the same anxious tone as before.

'I do remember it,' I answered, and I thought at the same moment, that it was a great pity the little maid had been kept in such ignorance. It was blissful ignorance in the present, but if the awakening came suddenly, it might be very terrible in the future.

But I felt that by the foregoing conversation I had bound myself to cleave to the fortunes of these girls until I could do them no further good. Poor patient Tessie, carrying her heavy burthen of disgrace alone, and lighthearted, unconscious Ange, dancing along the path of life as gaily as if it were all flowers and hid no secret mine which might explode at any moment and devastate her whole young, fresh existence : I could not tell which of the two I loved the more, nor which I could have the heart to forsake the sooner.

CHAPTER IX.

CHARLIE.

My compact with Tessie did not, however, preclude one thing, and that was the taking advice of my friends on the state of my affairs. With the state of those of other people I had nothing to do. But I could not decide whether to write to Mr. Warrington or Mrs. Sandilands. The solicitor was, of course, the most proper person to consult on the subject, but it appeared to be such a formidable proceeding to make a regular complaint to him, and I dreaded its entailing legal inquiries, and perhaps a complete estrangement between myself and the Lovetts. And, in that case, what would become of my promise of fidelity to Tessie? Mrs. Sandilands, on the other hand, although only a woman, had thorough good sense, and had managed all her own money affairs since her husband's death, and might be able to give me some hints by which to manage my guardian and obviate the necessity of calling in professional assistance.

So the day after I had taken that walk with Tessie, I sat down to write to Mrs. Sandilands. It was always a pleasure to me to take up the pen to address my old friend. Thoughts of the pretty countrified home which we had shared together, and of the many happy hours we had passed in each other's society, used to flow in upon me as I wielded it, and sometimes I was almost tempted to regret I had been so cold-hearted as to be unable to claim the title of daughter so warmly offered to me. What a cheerful, comfortable fireside theirs was. I could imagine no brighter lot for some poor lonely unloved orphan than to be welcomed to the bosom of the Sandilands family—for any orphan, that is to say, except Hilda Marsh. The bright-eyed helpful girls and the boisterous healthy boys, with their rosy cheeks and young clear voices—I fancied I could see them at that moment gathered round the dinner-table.

Nellie and Connie and Flo helping their mother to carve, whilst Bell, the spoilt baby of the family, albeit ten years old, was seated at Mrs. Sandilands' elbow, ready to grab at anything that came within her reach; and the boys' eyes were glistening at the sight of pudding, and their mouths, luckily for all those concerned, too full to permit them to make much noise.

Poor Charlie would not be present at that early meal. He always took his lunch in town, and relied on his mother looking after his creature comforts at tea-time.

Poor Charlie! I always thought of his name with that prefix, though I used to tell myself it was very ridiculous to do so; and that if he had inherited any of his mother's practical good sense, he must have seen, even before I had left Norwood, that the proposal he had made to me was one that, under any circumstances, I could never have entertained.

It was not his paltry income, nor the small chance he had of increasing it. If I loved a man, I felt that I could work for him, cooking dinners or scrubbing floors every day of my life, and be happier so, a great deal, than unloved and alone. But the one I slaved for must be superior to me. And poor Charlie was not. There was no conceit in saying so

—it was the veritable fact. He was a dear good old boy, and I felt sure that some day he would make some woman very happy indeed ; but it could never be myself.

Our natures didn't coalesce. I was too clear-sighted concerning him for any chance to remain of my friendship ripening into love. I saw so much too plainly that his hair was sandy and his moustaches nearly red, and that he had no idea of argument, and was uncomfortable in society, and appeared as though he had been unused to it.

Still I wished he had written to me. During the three months I had spent in St. Pucelle, though Mrs. Sandilands had sent me a letter almost every week, she had never enclosed more than a message from her son ; and I was curious about him, as all women are about their lovers, and wanted to find out if he had forgotten me, or was still silly enough to fret because I would not settle down in the bosom of his family as Mrs. Sandilands the Second.

What induced me to think about him so much that morning I do not know; but amongst my psychological studies, I have often observed the curious manner in which coming events often cast their shadow on the brain. Anyway, I was still sitting over that sheet of paper, nibbling my pen, and thinking of Charlie, when some one knocked at my bedroom door.

'All right!' I called out, imagining it to be a summons to *goûter*. 'I'm very glad it's ready, for I'm as hungry as I can be.'

'But no,' replied Ange's merry voice, in French, 'you are an hour out of your reckoning, Hilda: it is only half-past eleven. I come to tell you that somebody is waiting for you in the *salle*.'

'Somebody! That means that old bore

Miss Markham or her bosom friend Mrs. Carolus. No, thank you, *petite* Ange! I am writing a letter, and cannot be disturbed. Say you could see me nowhere. That will be quite true.'

' But supposing it is not Miss Markham or Miss Carolus! Suppose it is a gentleman, Hilda!'

My thoughts flew at once to Monsieur de Nesselrode, and my cheeks flamed like fire. That was because, since he had left off spending his evenings at our house, I had always felt a degree of guilty fear respecting him, under the idea that Mr. Lovett would some day question him too closely concerning his defalcation, and draw from him, perhaps against his will, a relation of the circumstances under which he had come to the determination to give up cards.

I felt the awkward position that in such a case I should be placed: of how impossible it would be for me to explain to my trustee that I had had Tessie's welfare at heart, more than that of the Baron, in persuading him to give up play, and that in going against the father's wishes, I had been doing my very best for the daughter. Mr. Lovett would say, and naturally think, that he knew what would secure his child's happiness better than myself, and I had no right to interfere. It would be very difficult to convince him that, beyond the pity which all right-minded people must feel to see a fellow creature throwing away his chances of happiness in this world, I had had no motive in advising the Baron to secure his. So that the name of De Nessselrode was rather a bugbear to me at that time; and I always felt my best safety lay in being present, if possible, at his interviews with Mr. Lovett.

So, on hearing Ange's last piece of intelligence, I threw my half-finished letter into my blotting-case, and smoothed my hair before the looking-glass.

'You need not wait, Ange. I will be down directly!' I exclaimed.

'Ah, I thought *that* would bring you, mademoiselle!' she called out with such a merry laugh, as she ran down the corridor, that I stopped short with the brush in my hand, to consider whether *petite* Ange had not been having a little amusement at my expense, and I should find myself in the arms of Mrs. Carolus after all. However, I resolved to go and see.

I followed her so quickly, that I caught her up in our little sitting-room, tying back her hair with a black ribbon.

'He's such a *nice* young man!' she said demurely; 'and Tessie is making such violent love to him already!'

'Ange, what a goose you are! I know it is only the Baron!'

'Well, go and see for yourself. If it is the Baron, he has dyed his hair!'

I opened the door of the *salle* quietly and looked in. No, it was decidedly not the Baron. That light-grey tweed suit and stuck-up collar never belonged to any one but an Englishman.

Ah, I had it now! It was my young friend of the steamboat—Mr. Charteris's cousin, Frederick Stephenson. I advanced quickly to bid him welcome. He turned round, and proved to be—Charlie Sandilands!

Oh, I *was* so pleased to see him! All the blood in my body, I verily believe, rushed to my face as I darted forward with both hands outstretched to grasp his.

'Charlie!' I exclaimed eagerly. 'Oh, Charlie, my dear old boy! wherever did you spring from?'

'I thought you would be surprised to see

me, Hilda,' he replied, with his eyes fixed upon my countenance; 'but I couldn't help coming—I couldn't, upon my word! I've got my annual leave, you see; and I did want to see you so much, that I put off taking it until I could spend it in St. Pucelle.'

'Oh, how good of you, Charlie! And how long will you be here?'

'Nearly a month, Hilda, unless you are sick of me before that time—in which case I shall go back to Norwood.'

'Sick of you? That's very likely! Why, it's like old times to see your face again! What jolly days we will have together! I am so glad you came before the fine weather was over. Isn't it a lovely place! And where are you staying, Charlie?'

In the gladness of my heart at meeting the boy again, I had been holding his hands all this time; but now, perceiving that Mr. Charteris was lounging in one of the window-seats, smoking, and regarding my ebullitions of delight, as I thought, with rather a contemptuous air, I dropped them as if they had been hot coals, and sat down on a chair close by.

'I have put up at the Hôtel d'Etoile,' said Charlie.

His pronunciation was delicious—something to make one scream by-and-by; but at that moment he might have stood on his head, and I should have regarded him gravely, so eager was I for news from my dear old home.

'That is all right. I am glad you have chosen the Etoile. It is nearer us than the Cloche. Fancy, I was just writing a letter to your dear mother, and thinking so much of you, Charlie, and all the others, when they knocked at my door to tell me you were here! I suppose you have been introduced to Miss Lovett?'

'Yes, Mr. Charteris was good enough to do so. I was surprised to see Charteris here, too, Hilda. It is quite a meeting of the clans! What an age it seems since he was at Norwood!'

Then I remembered that these two must have met at that period, though Charlie had been such a mere lad, that Mr. Charteris and I had doubtless considered that he had neither eyes nor ears. The recollection, however, of what I had told him of my early disappointment came back so vividly upon my mind, that I flushed scarlet and hated myself for so flushing, for fear lest the one man should interpret my change of countenance as regret for our lost intimacy, and the other accept it as a clue to the mysterious history I had partly confided to him. But Charlie appeared to see no connection at all in the two circumstances.

'Mr. Charteris had quite forgotten me,' he

went on, 'but I suppose that is not surprising. Hair upon one's face makes such a difference.' (Charlie's moustaches resembled the down on an apple-tart, and had to be caught sideways to be seen at all.) 'But I knew him at once. He is not the least altered since he was at Norwood. Is he, Hilda?'

'Men alter less at Mr. Charteris's age than they do at yours, Charlie. But tell me about your mother, and your brothers and sisters. I wish you could have brought your dear mother with you. And how are Nellie and Connie and Flo and little Bell? It seems years instead of months since I saw them all.'

'Oh, they're flourishing, Hilda, and going on just as usual. Nell's been worrying mother ever since you left to send her to a continental school, but I don't think she'll get her way. Mother's much too timid to let any one of them out of her sight.'

'There are no young ladies' schools in St. Pucelle, or I should try and persuade Mrs. Sandilands to send Nell here—and I'd look after her! It is so charming to see any one from the old country when you are exiled in a foreign land.'

'One would imagine to hear you talk, Miss Marsh,' interposed Mr. Charteris, 'and to see the rapture with which you welcome your friends from England, that you had been expatriated for a lifetime, instead of three months.'

He spoke 'nastily' to me, and he meant me to take it so. I could almost have thought, from the expression of his voice, that he was annoyed at witnessing the friendly terms on which I was with Charlie Sandilands. But that would have been too ridiculous, under the circumstances. However, I could not help giving him a *quid pro quo*.

'I am not in the habit of forgetting my

friends, Mr. Charteris. And if an absence of three months can make me so glad to meet them again, it is only a proof that I have found none better to take their places in the interim.'

He bit his lip and went on smoking, whilst I turned my attention again to Charlie, and continued my catechism of his home affairs.

It was strange that during the three weeks Cave Charteris and I had spent under the same roof, not a word nor a hint had been exchanged between us relating to our former intimacy. That he had entirely forgotten it I could not believe; neither could he credit me with so short a memory. On the contrary, his studied avoidance of the subject convinced me that he remembered only too well, although it was convenient to attribute his reticence to his fear of hurting my feelings by reviving thoughts of my lost mother.

At the same time he never appeared quite at his ease when in my presence, and as he reminded me painfully of a time of weakness and suffering which I had lived to be very much ashamed of, we had mutually avoided each other as much as possible. I was surprised, therefore, to see that he condescended to take any notice of my interest in Charlie Sandilands.

'Have you had luncheon yet, Charlie?' I went on, with my back turned to Mr. Charteris.

'No, Hilda. They told me at the hotel it was served at one.'

'Well, go and get it then, and come back to take a walk with me.'

'I shall be delighted!'

'Will not Mr. Sandilands stay and take some *goûter* with us, Hilda? Papa will be in directly,' interposed Tessie.

'*No!*' I said decidedly. 'He had better go back to his hotel.'

I had no idea of a friend of mine breaking bread in Mr. Lovett's house, whilst I could prevent it. The Sandilands had always been honest to the core. Let Charlie go and eat bread that had been paid for! I felt sure his mother would have said the same.

'Call for me at two o'clock,' I said in parting. 'I will take you such a lovely walk as you have never seen before, right up the hill to the forest of Piron.'

'Past the Château des Roses!' said Tessie, mischievously.

Ah! how she would have altered her tone, had she known *why* I took any interest in the Château des Roses or its master!

'Tessie, how can you!' I cried, with burning cheeks. 'Now, I shall take Mr. Sandilands in exactly the opposite direction, over the trout stream and through the valley of Artois!'

'But I saw that as I came in the diligence yesterday,' said Charlie.

'Then there are a dozen other walks, all prettier than the one I first mentioned, for me to introduce you to. But I want to take you right away from the town to some place where we can talk privately of all that has happened since we last met.'

'In three months!' sneered Cave Charteris.

When I say he 'sneered,' I mean that he spoke the words unpleasantly, and as though he would have liked to laugh, had he dared, at what I said.

'And why not?' I returned. 'A great deal of consequence may occur in that time. It is long enough to make or mar a life; why should I not find sufficient has happened in it to interest my friend for the length of a walk?'

'Everything that happens to you is of

interest to me, Hilda,' exclaimed Charlie, with boyish fervour.

'I knew that before I spoke! Mr. Charteris must have few friends worthy the name if he did not know it also!'

'I am not so fortunate as Miss Marsh,' replied that gentleman. 'No one takes such an interest in me.'

'Not those at home,' remarked Ange, pitifully. The little maid had crept into the *salle* a few minutes after myself. Charteris turned and looked searchingly into her blushing face.

'No, I am afraid not even "those at home," Miss Lovett. But how can I expect it? I am not Miss Hilda Marsh.'

'Even I have been forgotten by those I thought my friends,' I remarked quietly.

'But never by my mother nor me,' said Charlie, in an eager tone.

'I know that, Charlie, without your telling

me. But now go back to the hotel and get your *goûter*, and I will be ready for walking on your return.'

'How I wish some one would take me for a walk,' observed Mr. Charteris, with a professional sigh, as Charlie disappeared. *Petite* Ange said nothing, but she sighed also.

END OF VOL. II.

BILLING AND SONS, PRINTERS, GUILDFORD, SURREY.

www.ingramcontent.com/pod-product-compliance
Lightning Source LLC
Chambersburg PA
CBHW020805230426

43666CB00007B/860